To: Mike

Sept 20, 2000

Jae - Jin Kim
김 재 진 드림

DJ Welfarism

A New Paradigm for Productive Welfare in Korea

DJ Welfarism

A New Paradigm for Productive Welfare in Korea

Written by:
Office of the President
Republic of Korea
Presidential Committee for Quality-of-Life

Publishing Date: January 2000.
Publisher: Tae Sul Dang
Address: 494-9 Yongkang-dong, Mapo-gu, Seoul, Korea
Tel: (02) 701-1056
Fax: (02) 701-1057
Registration No: No. 7-368
Price: ₩7,000
ISBN: 89-85946-33-1

Office of the President
Republic of Korea
Presidential Committee for Quality-of-Life

FOREWORD

As the new millennium approaches, the Korean people are optimistic about the future of the country. The past century has been an era of both agony and glory. The nation has endured 36 years of colonial rule, a devastating war, and most recently a financial crisis. Despite these hardships, the country has risen from abject poverty to now being the world's 11th largest economy. In the early 1960s, annual per capita income was less than $100. By 1997, annual per capita income had risen to more than $10,000. Within a relatively short span of 30 years, Korea has emerged from economic obscurity to now having a presence within the circle of highly advanced countries.

Although South Korea has had extraordinary economic success, the country still suffers from a legacy of authoritarian rule which prioritized economic growth at the expense of economic and political democracy. Big business was allocated an undue share of the nation's resources while smaller companies were relegated to merely serving the needs of the country's large conglomerates. Dictatorial rule suppressed political democracy and ignored economic democracy, which resulted in a wide gap between the rich and the poor and a lack of any guarantee of human rights.

Throughout the 1980s, the people struggled for political reform, which often led to severe government repression. In 1987, however, provisions were established to hold direct elections for the nation's president. The promise of the 1987 election reform was fulfilled in 1993 with the first truly democratic election of a Korean president. Five years later, in 1998, the nation again demonstrated its firm commitment to democracy by electing a new president, who was from the opposition party. The smooth transition of power from one party to another was another striking demonstration of the fact that democracy had taken firm root in the land, even though broad-based democracy had never before been in the public lexicon of political life.

When I became the president of Korea in 1998, I vowed to myself that I would live up to the nation's expectations that I should resolve the conflicts that continue to persist as a legacy of Korea's past. We have, thus far, had some successes, but there is still much to be done to rectify the economic and social injustices of the past. The financial crisis of 1997 exposed many of Korea's weaknesses, but with the cooperative efforts of the international community, our nation was able to navigate through the crisis. On behalf of the Korean people, I thank the international community for their friendship and their help.

One of the weaknesses of Korea's past preoccupation with growth at the expense of democracy and human rights is the wide gap that still exists between the rich and the poor. In the past, large domestic corporate conglomerates were allocated a disproportionately large share of the nation's resources, which relegated smaller enterprises to merely serving the needs of the very large corporations. These government-imposed inequities created regional and class conflicts that continue to erode social unity. Since the 1950s, I have supported balanced economic development that is based on economic democracy under which market forces would determine the allocation of resources and economic opportunity would be available to all, not just a few. The fruit of prosperity should be shared by all citizens, which means that people who work hard should be rewarded accordingly. A fair, or equitable, distribution of wealth exemplifies the concept of economic democracy. Fairness instills mutual trust among all strata of society and assures that human dignity is enjoyed by all citizens.

Our objective in fulfilling the promise of economic democracy entails the reshaping of the Korean economy to make it more responsive to the demands of the marketplace while being sensitive to the needs of employees and the interests of the nation. Since 1997, Korea has attempted to eliminate the entrenched government — business collusion, which was responsible for a lack of fiscal discipline and inequalities in the distribution of wealth across geographic regions of the country. The financial crisis imposed fiscal restraints on the Government and subjected the big conglomerates to the need to reduce their unwieldy debts. The effort to correct these conditions and the new policies administered by the Administration led to rapid recovery so that the nation's foreign currency reserves are now at an all-time record high, the economic growth rate is rising, and unemployment is decreasing.

Despite our recent successes, however, there are still unresolved problems in our society. There is a relatively large number of long-term unemployed workers. Employment has become unstable as more and more companies hire an increasing number of part-time or temporary workers. The inequitable distribution of wealth that is a legacy of the past has led to an increase in the number of people that live below the poverty line. Thus, the time has come for us to create economic and social conditions which will ensure that all citizens can enjoy a minimum standard of living.

Now is the time to formulate a government policy that will provide for more of the benefits of economic recovery reaching the middle and lower classes who have suffered from bankruptcies, unemployment, and income loss resulting from corporate restructuring. The social inequity that government policy must address results from the fact that these socioeconomic groups have been less rewarded for their economic contributions to society than have the more privileged strata of Korean society. Before the financial crisis, the lower strata of society did not always receive their fair share of prosperity. After the onset of the crisis, the middle and lower classes were subjected to even more serious income disruption as businesses began to restructure to prepare for a more productive future. The middle and lower classes, however, are the backbone of a stable society and their productive work should be fairly rewarded. Our challenge is to provide the framework for everyone across all socioeconomic strata to realize a minimum standard of living and be equitably rewarded for their work, while encouraging corporate restructuring that often results in a reduction of the workforce. Society needs and should value the contributions of all its citizens. If each and every citizen cannot share in the prosperity of society as a whole, then the nation will not be able to achieve sustainable economic and social development in the new millennium.

During the years of struggle to democratize Korea, I began to realize that national economic prosperity is not the only ingredient of a healthy society. Although a minimum standard of living is important, the quality of life for all citizens in the national community is equally important if society is to avert social fragmentation and discord across socioeconomic class lines. In the context of political democracy, a balance must be struck between market economics and the redistribution of wealth. Such a balance aims at minimizing the alienation of those who cannot adequately compete in a free, competitive market. To equitably distribute wealth while not stifling initiative and entrepreneurship, I propose the concept of "productive welfare," which is the foundation of government policies that cater to the demands of sustained economic growth, while providing for the sharing of economic prosperity among all citizens.

The productive welfare policy rejects the simple notion of passively protecting the poor and the disadvantaged by merely giving them money. Passive welfare does not elevate a recipient's sense of self-worth nor does the simple giving of alms create opportunities for economic and social advancement. A more proactive approach to welfare is for the Government to provide the means for self-improvement and, ultimately, self-support.

I declare the year 2000 to be the first year in which we actively pursue productive welfare. By doing so, we can transform a complementary system of economic democracy and market economics into a productive system of welfare. I envision a society in which everyone has the means to improve themselves through education and training, everyone has a chance to develope his or her talents, everyone is paid fairly according to his or her contribution, and everyone enjoys the benefits of a healthy and prosperous society. I am positive that implementing productive welfare will help our nation realize a high standard of living across the socioeconomic spectrum while respecting and guaranteeing individual human rights.

Another legacy of Korea's past growth-first strategy is the pollution of the environment. Rivers, lakes, and streams have been environmentally abused by the dumping of toxic materials and waste. Noxious emissions from factories and refineries and the burning of vehicle fuels have contaminated the air we breathe. Water and air pollution are killing fish and birds, which threatens our food supply. Productive welfare aims at eradicating this blight by implementing policies that discourage the abuse of the environment, while encouraging all sectors of society to be environmentally sensitive. Our goal is to harmonize the needs of society with the preservation of nature to assure sustainable growth.

The implementation of productive welfare entails the structuring of administrative procedures and mechanisms that fairly distribute economic output within the framework of a market economy and fairly reward those who participate in productive activities. To foster the long-term health of the economy, government intervention will be needed to help those who are temporarily excluded from the labor market. Providing a means for these workers to be re-employed is viewed by the concepts of productive welfare as an obligation of the Government. An often neglected segment of society is the permanently unemployed who have lost hope and face despair and low self-esteem. Rather than dismissing these people as losses, productive welfare seeks ways for them to become socially productive. Embracing everyone in society into the realm of productivity assures a higher degree of social integration across all socioeconomic strata.

Productive welfare also recognizes the hazards of life that any person in society can encounter. A national pension system has recently been installed to protect the welfare of the elderly. Universal medical insurance is very important for the welfare of citizens of all ages. Employment insurance is a means to provide welfare for those who are temporarily unemployed. Industrial accident protection helps to maintain a productive workforce. In implementing these welfare programs, productive welfare recognizes that safeguards must be built into the system to discourage abuse, which is tantamount to nonproductive almsgiving. The major objective in all of these programs is to ensure self-sufficiency despite intervening setbacks.

The world is becoming smaller and smaller as transportation and communications technology continue their relentless advance. International commerce has become highly interdependent and national borders are becoming less and less important in the conduct of business. Consequently, the poverty and inequitable distribution of wealth within developing countries have now become the problems of the entire world. To resolve these problems, we cannot rely solely on the principles of democracy and market economics. We must seek ways to implement the concept of productive welfare on a multinational plane if each individual nation is to fully enjoy the benefits that advances in technology, especially information technology, can yield.

My hope is that the idea of productive welfare, described in this book, will become a model of development for other countries who must raise their standards of living. I am especially hopeful that other Asian countries can benefit by Korea's experience. Raising the living standards of all nations in the region would narrow the economic and social gaps that currently exist among these nations and would most assuredly reduce the risk of destructive conflict.

I am confident that Korea will be remembered as the nation that created an exemplary society where a balance of material growth and social welfare provided productive opportunities for self-fulfillment and where the rewards of prosperity were equitably distributed to all citizens.

Kim Dae-jung
President of the Republic of Korea
January 2000

PREFACE

The Kim Dae-jung Administration, dubbed the "Government of the People," has achieved much progress in forging Korea's economic recovery since the onset of the foreign exchange crisis in late 1997. The Administration has prepared the groundwork for a market economy through the continuous support of restructuring, despite numerous problems that have emerged during the Administration's implementation of structural reform. As adjustments were made to the economic and political structure of the nation, the daily lives of the general population became more difficult. Unemployment rose sharply and a deterioration in the equitable distribution of income quickly emerged. As unemployment rose, confrontation between labor and management weakened the level of social integration.

In order to achieve a more fair distribution of wealth and to improve relations among all strata of society, a policy of sustained economic development must now be pursued. To this end, President Kim Dae-jung has introduced the concept of "productive welfare" into his Administration along with the principles of democracy and market economics.

President Kim first introduced the concept of productive welfare in an article entitled "Direction of the Labor Movement in Korea," which was published in the Korean journal, Sasang-Gae in 1955. Since then, he has reiterated the concept of productive welfare in such books as Mass-Participatory Economy (1997) and DJnomics (1998). In August 1999, President Kim again advocated the productive welfare concept in a speech he made to celebrate Korea's 54th Liberation Day, declaring that he would implement a policy of productive welfare which would "maintain individual dignity and raise the living standards of all Koreans."

This book has been written to enunciate President Kim's concept of productive welfare. We acknowledge the assistance of many people from various universities, research institutes, and civic organizations who made this book possible, either by personally contributing to the writing of the manuscript or by advising on the book's structure and contents. We hope that the publication of this book will foster a better understanding of the concept of productive welfare. We are confident that Korea will become an advanced nation in the 21st Century, where both social and economic development will be equally important.

Kim, Yoo Bae
Senior Secretary to the President
for Welfare and Labor

January 2000

Contents

Part I

Philosophy and Vision

In his Liberation Day speech in August 1999, President Kim Dae-jung elaborated his notion of productive welfare and the direction toward which he is leading the nation, stating that "we need a system of productive welfare where each person can put forth his or her best efforts for social development, while sharing both the community's successes and its failures." He also promised to foster the continued development of democracy and to expand the institutions of market economics as part of the national philosophy. Mr. Kim also promised to "actively introduce productive welfare policies that are incentive based and which aim at fostering the growth of the middle class and improving the standard of living for all Koreans.

Productive welfare is a part of President Kim's overall plan to overcome the recent financial crisis that plagued Korea as well as other Asian nations. Under other elements of the President's plan, socioeconomic policies that can improve the basic standard of living of the middle class and the Korean people in general will be actively pursed. The main focus of President Kim's Administration is, thus, to guarantee basic human rights and to improve the quality of life, issues that had previously been neglected by authoritarian administrations which focused only on modernizing Korea.

Chapter 1

Background of Productive Welfare

The continued development of democracy and a market economy has made possible the surmounting of Korea's recent economic crisis and promises to construct a bright future for the new millennium. Productive welfare will be instrumental in establishing Korea as an advanced nation in the 21st Century, which will assure a high quality of life for the Korean people. Productive welfare recognizes that concern for the welfare of the nation's citizens was neglected in the process of promoting rapid economic growth. Productive welfare is, therefore, based upon the need to strengthen social integration which has been weakened by an inequitable distribution of income and high unemployment that was precipitated at the onset of the financial crisis of 1997.

1. From Unbalanced to Balanced Development

Since the 1960s, small- and medium-sized enterprises in Korea have not grown substantially, primarily because of the national economic policy of prioritizing rapid growth. Most of these smaller enterprises have been reduced to the role of subcontractor or have remained as small-scale businesses because much of Korea's energy focused on large conglomerates, or "chaebol." The agricultural sector still lags behind the urban sector in terms of living standards. In many outskirts of urban areas, people are living in poverty, while the urban middle class enjoys a high standard of living.

This lack of regional balance in development has become aggravated by an unequal allocation of resources imposed by past authoritarian political regimes. Creativity in business and efficient management, based on accountability, had been neglected because of the pernicious practice of government — business collusion. Companies sought monopolistic interests through collaboration with those in power instead of relying on the principles of market economics. As a result of this process, economic growth was achieved, but at the cost of skewed allocations of the nation's resources, which culminated in the imposition of monetary, fiscal, and structural reforms by the International Monetary Fund (IMF) in 1997.

The rights and interests of the socially underprivileged,

4

including low-income laborers and small businesses, were not sufficiently protected because of a policy that prioritized growth first, while leaving the equitable distribution of wealth as a secondary concern. The subsistence level of the under-privileged declined to a very low point, and the poor had to rely heavily on charity for sustenance. Consequently, a strategy for balanced social development must be established to resolve social discrimination and alienation so that all people may enjoy a better quality of life.

2. Importance of Social Integration and Overcoming the Economic Crisis

Until 1997, most Koreans believed that full employment and rapid economic growth were both attainable. That confidence fizzled away, however, after the economic crisis. People realized that the collapse of the economy would be inevitable unless a free and competitive market was esta-blished.

People rejected the authoritarian regimes of the past and a new government that focuses on people was elected by the voters in a smooth transition of power from one political party to another. Concurrently, the general public seemed to be excited in helping to develop democracy and a market economy. President Kim's Administration was, thus, successful in rescuing the national economy from economic crisis by responding to the demands of the people. As a result of the Administration's efforts, foreign currency reserves have remarkably recovered to higher levels than before the crisis and a favorable trade balance has been maintained, all occurring with rising economic growth and declining unemployment.

All is not bright, however. Social integration seems to be deteriorating as the economy recovers. A high rate of unemployment has appeared and employment is no longer stable. The number of people earning low wages is rising and the distribution of wealth is becoming less equitable.

To resolve these problems, there must be some change in current social policies to restore the weakened social dynamics that currently exist within a constantly changing economic environment. Productive welfare will attempt to correct Korea's weak welfare system and the deterioration of basic human rights, caused by the quantitative growth policies of the past, while developing a system that nurtures both growth and equitable income distribution.

Chapter 2

Philosophical Foundation
of Productive Welfare

1. Welfare and Human Rights

The recognition of human rights and citizenship as encompassing a system of welfare, as well as a complementary recognition of the responsibility of the state, form the philosophical premise of the Kim Dae-jung Administration. In the context of rights, this means that all people have the right to enjoy life, health, and culture. The converse obligation is on the state to guarantee and protect those rights.

The recognition of social welfare as a basic human right has been the result of decades of relentless efforts to expand the boundaries of human rights. The rights movement began with a struggle to secure civil rights, such as personal freedom and the freedoms of speech, conscience, and thought. The rights movement then proceeded to secure political rights, and later, economic rights. Rights activists soon came to realize, however, that unenforceable rights are no rights at all and, consequently, redirected their objective toward securing active freedoms as opposed to passive freedoms.

Social welfare as a civil right forms the basis of the modern welfare society which presupposes that welfare is a right, rather than an occasional act of benevolence. The individual in modern society is not only an economic entity participating in the market, but is also a human member of society, of the nation.

While the market should be free to operate efficiently through the interaction of supply and demand, such interaction overlooks the many needs of those who are unable to compete in the market, whether through old age, young age, disability, or some other vulnerability. Regardless of their ability or inability to compete in the market, the vulnerable still retain their rights: their right to life, to minimum living standards, to minimum education, to healthcare, and to housing.

The Constitution is legally the highest law in the Republic of Korea, regulating not only the behavior of its citizens but also of its government. Article 10 stipulates that all people must be guaranteed human dignity and the right to pursue happiness. The Constitution also places an obligation on the Government to ensure that those rights are protected and that they are enforced. These constitutional rights were, however, never been translated into real rights, because economic growth and development had consistently been prioritized over welfare. The injection of productive welfare concepts into the policies of the Kim Dae-jung Administration, thus, endeavors to give effect to these constitutional rights, which previous administrations had failed to do.

2. Welfare and the Right to Work

Productive welfare begins with the recognition of human rights as central to human existence and ends with the principle of "welfare through work." The welfare policy pursued by the Kim Dae-jung Administration replaces the traditional passive model of welfare with a dynamic model of welfare through which the right to work will be guaranteed.

Work is not only a means of earning a living, but is an essential means of attaining a sense of satisfaction and value, *i.e.* attaining dignity. Productive welfare recognizes the importance of socioeconomic participation, and accordingly, takes "the right to work" seriously. With regard to people who have been alienated from socioeconomic activities, the right to work implies that they must be given the means to enhance their opportunities and their capabilities to actively participate in the labor market.

Welfare through work addresses the need for a balance between the too often conflicting principles of the market and of welfare, while overcoming the limitations of existing welfare policies that rely on the Government's policy of redistribution. In looking back, the 20th Century paradigm for welfare was a straightforward model that involved the simple redistribution of wealth. Conversely, a laissez-faire culture ensured that the marketplace became a battleground for the survival of the fittest and, consequently, a place devoid of concerns for welfare.

Neither simple redistribution nor laissez-faire policies, however, can support sustainable economic development in the 21st Century. The profusion of conflicting demands from government, the market, and welfare can only lead to a breakdown of society. A delicate and responsive balance, in which each sector responds to the needs of the others and minimum living standards for all are guaranteed, can, however, ensure the continued development of society. From this perspective, welfare policies can be viewed as an investment for improved productivity, rather than as a simple transfer of income through administrative procedures.

One place where the market, government, and welfare

converge is employment. Government policies of simple redistribution cannot continue to encumber capital resources in response to the increasing growth of welfare demands that are produced by market failure. There are several ways in which government can fulfil its policy-imposed responsibility to assure a basic standard of living for the underprivileged with minimum intervention: First, by bringing the unemployed back into the labor market by providing opportunities to find new jobs. Second, the underprivileged who have never been in the workforce can be provided with opportunities to perform productive work. The objective is to include everyone in the workforce, regardless of ability, disability, deprivation, or privilege.

An active policy of welfare through work is imperative in view of two global changes that may undermine the right to work. The first is globalization. Because of the increase in the worldwide volume of foreign investments, national boundaries in terms of investment have blurred as competition among businesses is now played out on a global rather than domestic scale. The implication for employment is that businesses may be forced to cut labor costs in order to enhance productivity if they are to survive fierce global competition. An active model of welfare is able to respond to this new environment with policies that nurture the skills necessary to match the changing demands of the labor market.

Pursuing active welfare policies, *e.g.* the development and training of the labor force and the expansion of opportunities offered to the labor force, will generate a form of social capital, that is, "labor power," which can be invested into future businesses. This complementary interaction between the market and welfare through work, then plays a central role in the theory of productive welfare.

The second global change threatening the security of employment is the technological revolution, which has ushered in the Information Age. This change is shifting the industrial structure of developed countries from manufacturing-based industries to information-based industries. These rapidly evolving technological changes will reduce the value of skills currently possessed by workers; thus, finding and maintaining adequate employment will become increasingly difficult for those who cannot adapt to the technological changes. To protect the right to work, the Government must not only protect existing jobs, but must help to create new jobs by dealing flexibly with the changing demands of the labor market. The Government must also support workers by continually providing opportunities for education and training, so that workers themselves are able to respond to the new demands of the Information Age.

3. Welfare and Social Integration

Productive welfare is predicated on reaching consensus among the government, the market, and society. To this end, social integration among all members of the community is essential along with a guarantee of human rights and the right to work.

Social integration has always played an important role in society, creating the necessary community spirit to assist and protect the less privileged. Community spirit was traditionally prevalent among members of the same tribe, village communities, and religious organizations and was expressed through acts of kindness. These communal ties gradually weakened with the advent of individual-oriented secular society and capitalism. The weakening of social ties was exacerbated by the fact that care for the socially vulnerable came to be the responsibility of the public sector, as a result of the disproportionate emphasis placed on individualism and competition.

Within Korea's own traditions, there were several expressions of social unity, such as: Hyang-yak, which means self-sufficiency or communal management of the country village; the Du-re which refers to a farmer's cooperative group; and Gu-hyul, which refers to communal assistance. These traditions, however, were destroyed in the process of rapid modernization. Currently, the possibilities for a new system of social integration that are suitable for modern society are being explored. The activities of various civic organizations, for example, non-government organizations (NGOs), local community groups, and religious organizations, have been expanding since the democratization of Korea and show signs of hope for a revival of community spirit among the entire Korean population.

The objective of the welfare system is ultimately to reconcile the differences between independence and inter-dependence. If mutual understanding and cooperation are as important as individual identity, then society will not exclude any one person from pursuing their identity. A new welfare model would, thus, proceed on the basis of co-operative participation by government, business, and society at large. A partnership could be implemented where the Government could take charge of certain services, such as healthcare, childcare, and protection of the poor, by supporting civic organizations and other NGOs. Businesses could in turn support non-profit charitable organizations. The part-nership of these three entities, the Government, society, and business, would not only contribute to the effective utilization of public assets, but would also contribute to the indepen-dence of the less privileged, who are unable to participate in the mainstream labor market, by providing them with a meaningful place to work.

The central system of welfare in which the central government controls the sphere and scope of welfare, must be decentralized to a local community-based system of welfare. Rather than depending solely on central-government funding, a more efficient and flexible local welfare system can be constructed to solve local problems by forming a partnership between governing organizations, businesses, and civic groups in the local community and by utilizing volunteer services in the local communities.

The construction of a welfare network at the local community level will first and foremost contribute to the independence of welfare recipients. A welfare network at the local community level will enable passive welfare recipients, who only receive benefits, to become active citizens, who participate in meaningful work as members of the local community. In this way, problems not only relating to material existence can be overcome, but also problems relating to social alienation.

4. Relationships among Democracy, Market Economics, and Productive Welfare

Productive welfare is not a simple addition to democracy and market economics but concurrently interacts with and solidifies these two elements of government. Previous authoritarian regimes in Korea restricted civil participation in the distribution of political, social, and economic resources. Fair distribution and welfare were not the primary concern of those administrations. Productive welfare, however, is an active attempt to enhance the development of democracy in Korea, from simple procedural democracy to an entrenched, functioning democracy, by actively facilitating socioeconomic democratization and meeting people's demands for welfare.

In making the transition from an authoritarian to a democratic form of government and from a centrally guided market economy to a market economy, legacies of abuse will inevitably remain. Politically, the privileged minority will still have greater participation in government, while the interests of the socially vulnerable will remain passive. Economically, the existing business structures, which were erected through government—business collusion, will attempt to ensure that many smaller businesses will continue to fall behind in the new competitive global environment. In both politics and economics, productive welfare will have a role to play on behalf of the interests of the socially vulnerable: by actively speaking for them, by providing economic assistance to them, and by minimizing conflict among them and other members of society.

Productive welfare is, thus, a core policy that forms the

framework for the Republic of Korea to become an advanced nation in the new millennium by preempting the possible tensions that may arise through the interaction of democracy and a market economy. The goal of Productive welfare is to promote harmonious development through sustained economic growth and broad-based democracy.

Chapter 3

Concept and Vision
of Productive Welfare

Productive welfare is an ideology, as well as a policy, that seeks to secure minimum living standards for all people, while expanding opportunities for self-support in socio-economic activities for the purpose of maintaining human dignity. As such, productive welfare endeavors to improve the quality of life for all citizens by promoting social development and a fair distribution of wealth.

1. Components of Productive Welfare

Productive welfare strives to build a society that improves the quality of life for all people, including the socially estranged, by encouraging the active economic participation of all people in the nation and by assuring a fair distribution of wealth. A fair, or equitable, distribution of wealth, must act as the framework for securing minimum living standards for all citizens, while stable economic growth must have complementary relationships that contribute to an improvement in the quality of life for everyone, not just for the few.

Thus, the theory of productive welfare is composed of primary distribution through an equitable market system, a fair redistribution of wealth by the Government for meeting basic human needs, social investment for self-support, and expansion of investment to enhance the quality of life for everyone in society.

1.1. Distribution Through an Equitable Market System

The first component of productive welfare is a fair labor market through which appropriate and fair working conditions can be achieved. Productive welfare assures that the quality of life can be improved by providing equal opportunities for all to participate in production and in the equitable distribution of capital in the marketplace. Equal opportunities must be offered to everyone. Workers must receive fair compensation for the work they do and discrimination, such as the unfair dismissal of the socially weak, must be abolished. Within a fair labor market, the middle class will be nurtured and will grow to include, for example laborers, farmers, and the self-employed.

1.2. Redistribution of Wealth by the Government

The second component of productive welfare is the re-distributive policy of the Government. The challenge is to secure minimum living standards for all people, allowing them to escape from poverty, alienation, and social risk. If the distribution of wealth is left to market forces alone, those who fail to keep pace with market competition will be overlooked, which will, in turn, result in social discontent and discord. Thus, government intervention through welfare policies is necessary to protect the interests of everyone.

Within the context of fair distribution, the aim of the Government is to maintain the dignity of all people. The Government must appropriately lessen the effects of poverty, disease, and a lack of educational opportunities to secure minimum standards of living. This function might be implemented through a more comprehensive social security system, which covers the entire population, and through policies of optimal protection and assistance for the under-privileged, including the aged, disabled, women, and the long-term unemployed, who have limited opportunities for social participation. Equitable redistribution would thereby contribute to strengthening social integration.

This redistributive function of the Government would provide those who are temporarily excluded from the market with the necessary relief to enable rapid reemployment and would allow those who are permanently excluded from the market to maintain minimum living standards. Equitable redistribution would thereby contribute to strengthened social integration.

To fund redistribution, a re-ordering of the tax system will be necessary. Many developed countries employ a progressive levy on personal income where the highest income earners pay the highest rate of taxes, while the lowest income bracket is exempt from taxation on personal income. Weaknesses of a progressive income tax have, however, appeared in some cases. If the rich are over-taxed, then capital investment is stifled and chronic economic stagnation results. If the rich are not taxed enough, then the middle class, primarily comprised of salaried workers, bears an unduly heavy burden of supporting the welfare system. A fair-minded balance must, therefore, be struck between providing incentives for capital investment and unduly high taxation of the middle class.

1.3. Social Investment for Self-Support

The third component of productive welfare is a welfare policy that encourages the self-support of the underprivileged. If the re-distributive policy of the Government simply hands out benefits without providing opportunities for people who have the ability to work, *i.e.* the ability to achieve self-support., then welfare recipients would be further estranged from mainstream society. An active welfare policy that provides vocational training, a variety of educational opportunities, and job creation programs would, thus, affirm and support people's right to work.

Productive welfare embraces the virtues of independence and self-support, which help to overcome social alienation and discrimination. Productive welfare is proactive, in that it supports the socially weak and impoverished to enable them to break out from the cycle of poverty and estrangement. The ultimate objective is to have the socially weak become self-supportive by including them in a market-based economy under an umbrella of social support. Through suitable education and training of the underprivileged, who are less able to compete in the mainstream market, productive welfare aims to restore the desire and the capability to work.

1.4. Expansion of Investment to Enhance the Quality of Life

Productive welfare is not complete with just equitable distribution of market opportunities and a redistribution policy securing minimum living standards. Because productive welfare ultimately pursues the enhancement of the quality of life for all people regardless of their places in society, it aims to provide people with social circumstances that facilitate access to education, health, environment and cultural occasions for their lifetime. Easy access to lifelong education may guarantee adaptation to changing conditions in a knowledge-based society. By the same token, better chances to enjoy healthcare, a living environment and cultural affairs will serve as an advanced form of welfare.

Without the Government's initiatives in social investment for improving the quality of life, some people may have to spend a large portion of their incomes to achieve better circumstances in education, healthcare, environment and culture in their lives. Accordingly, many people at the lower levels of social stratification would suffer from the costs of acquiring those commodities in the market. Productive welfare, therefore, aims to develop a social infrastructure which provides all people with more equitable opportunities to enjoy a better quality of life regardless of their social status. While investing a larger budget in this area, the government will try to fairly enhance the quality of life for everyone.

2. Sustainable Growth and Prosperity

Social equality cannot be achieved by the competitive market alone nor can welfare resources be sustained if welfare programs simply redistribute the fruits of economic growth. The dichotomies of market versus welfare and growth versus distribution can be accepted by all strata of society within the framework of productive welfare as a complementary set of values.

In this present age of intense global competition and information-based industrialization, sustainable growth will not be possible if the Government continues to rely upon a passive welfare system. Policies that influence the equitable distribution of resources in the marketplace must be complemented with a balanced distribution of welfare benefits that help individuals, as well as the nation.

Productive welfare will form the underlying framework of the Kim Administration's efforts to pursue policies based upon principles of democracy and market economics. The development of democracy must go beyond formal and legal recognition of human rights. The basic human rights of all individuals must be assured to include the socially alienated, including orphans, the disabled, and abandoned senior citizens. Similarly, the development of a market economy must move toward providing equal opportunities for all

24

people, to enable their participation in production and distribution processes.

The ultimate objective of productive welfare is to form a society in which all people can maintain their dignity and self-worth and in which a better quality of life can be attained by all people in society. The vision of productive welfare for the coming millennium is to construct a model nation in which ideologies, such as human rights, become a reality.

3. Global Implications of Productive Welfare

New global opportunities will emerge for the balanced development of democracy and a market economy, through productive welfare. Liberalization of international trade and intensification of economic interdependence among countries has occasioned the diffusion of economic and social problems into the international community, which have become more difficult to contain within the boundaries of any one country.

After experiencing a deterioration in national living standards and in social integration that was caused by the 1997 financial crisis, Korea has recognized that productive welfare is essential for assuring higher standards of living. From this productive welfare perspective, President Kim Dae-jung at the 1999 APEC Leaders Meeting in New Zealand proposed policies that induce joint prosperity through exchange and cooperation among countries in the Asia-Pacific region. Based upon the support and participation of these states, the Korean Government will endeavor to reduce the socioeconomic disparity among nations, which will be especially difficult to attain because of economic and knowledge-based disparities among nations in the region. International cooperation for education, including development of human resources through cyber-education, transfer of scientific technology, vocational training, and lifetime education, will be advocated.

The Kim Administration is currently formulating a plan to ensure a quality of life that will advance global harmony among all humanity, social systems, and the natural environment.

Part II

From National Minimum Living Standards to Quality of Life

Productive welfare seeks to secure a higher quality of life by protecting all people from various social risks. In this context, the Korean Government has placed a high priority on securing basic human rights and a minimum standard of living for people who currently are not able to lead self-supporting lives. Productive welfare, along with the development of a market economy, also allows for an improved quality of life through greater job opportunities and a more equitable distribution of wealth. The ultimate objective of a productive welfare policy is to create a society where citizens enjoy a high quality of life. The most important aspect of this effort is to create an arena in which all classes can cooperatively participate in the shaping of social policy issues for the benefit of all citizens. To reach this goal, the Government will form the framework for making available to all people in the nation, education, culture, and a healthfully clean environment.

Chapter 4

Welfare That Secures
National Minimum Living Standards

Productive welfare begins with the challenge to secure minimum living standards for all people, as cited in Mass -Participatory Economy (1997). If the minimum conditions necessary for the realization of a higher quality of life are not met because of social impediments, such as poverty, disease, unemployment, and inadequate housing, then promoting productive welfare policies of self-support through voluntary human development efforts and labor is impossible.

If any group does not share in the fruits of economic growth, development is deficient. Therefore, to ensure equal opportunity for the full participation of all groups, society has an obligation to provide basic necessities to those who cannot secure them independently. These people include the disabled, the disadvantaged, and the temporarily unemployed. However, in fulfilling this obligation, society must make sure that the recipients of its generosity do not neglect their obligation to society.

There are several policy goals that are required in any attempt to provide a minimum standard of living. First, a minimum standard of living should be secured to ensure that no one person lives below the poverty line. Where people without the ability to work have fallen into poverty, assistance will be provided to enable them to meet the minimum standard of living, while people with the ability to work will be assisted to become more independent. Through these efforts, the Government will attempt to guarantee a higher quality of life for the poor. Furthermore, by embracing economically alienated groups within society, greater social integration should be possible.

Second, through the expansion and strengthening of the social insurance system, the Government will seek to lessen the effects of social risks, for example disease, old age, and natural disaster. Korea has already established four major social insurance schemes, including the national pension system, health insurance, unemployment insurance, and industrial injury insurance. A more comprehensive national pension plan was established in April 1999 which expanded the coverage of the national pension system to the urban self-employed. Despite advancements, the entire population has yet to be covered by the social insurance system and the level of benefits are still insufficient. Thus, the social security system will be enhanced in order to provide greater stability in the face of unavoidable changes, such as those associated with the aging of the baby-boomer population and rapid socioeconomic reconfigurations.

Third, self-support plans will be diversified to assist the underprivileged. Self-support will be encouraged through various assistance programs, such as education, development of skills, and the provision of information. Diversified assistance will not only increase the degree of self-sufficiency, but will also enable a more stable participation in the economy by the underprivileged, thereby contributing to greater social integration.

1. Securing National Minimum Living Standards

Until now, national policies related to poverty have been based on the expansion of job opportunities through general economic growth. While these policies achieved a high level of economic growth and overall improvement in the quality of life, the distribution of the fruits of economic growth to low-wage earners has continued to be relatively insufficient.

The responsibility for addressing difficulties experienced by the underprivileged, such as the elderly and the disabled, had, consequently, been placed on the individual and the family. The hardships faced by the underprivileged have become worse since the economic crisis. Poverty has increased as a result of long-term unemployment, as is evident with greater visibility of the homeless and the increasingly larger number of children who are suffering from malnutrition. These conditions show that the problems of abject poverty, which were expected to be resolved through economic growth, still exist. Overcoming the perils of poverty has become even more difficult since the economic crisis. The present policy for protecting people on low incomes from the effects of poverty is inadequate, which is evident in the current absence of welfare benefits for people who have low incomes and who have the ability to work. The social welfare system, as it stands today, does not facilitate self-support as a means to escape from poverty.

1.1. Guarantee of Minimum Living Standards Through Legislation

The Minimum Living Standards Security Act was legislated in August 1999 in response to pleas from all sectors of society for reform of the former Living Protection Act. Passage of the reform act marked a transformation in the direction of welfare policies from a policy of simple giving of alms, as provided by the Living Protection Act, to a policy stressing national responsibility based on the rights of welfare recipients.

Starting from October 2000, the Government will ensure that basic needs, including food, clothing, housing, education, and healthcare, are met for all people living below minimum living standards. In other words, all households, whose incomes do not meet the minimum cost of living, will receive welfare benefits from the Government that equal the difference. Housing benefits will also be established to elevate housing assistance for the underprivileged. By implementing these benefits, the Government will seek to expand housing welfare policies by introducing minimum housing standards and increasing the supply of public housing.

The Minimum Living Standards Security Act (1999) will not only guarantee minimum living standards for all poor people, but will simultaneously provide welfare programs linked to labor. These provisions will enable people on low incomes who have the ability to work to become more self-supporting and independent. For example, low-wage earners with the ability to work who receive welfare benefits must also participate in job-training programs or other programs that contribute to the public good, such as public works. Providing these benefits, as an incentive to participate in the labor market, aims at reinforcing the independence of the Korean people and restoring their desire to work.

2. Strengthening the Social Insurance System

The social insurance system exists to protect people by guaranteeing their minimum living standards in old age, by lessening the effects of risks arising from economic uncertainties, and by minimizing the risks experienced by all people living in industrialized societies, including disease, unemployment, and industrial accidents. Although Korea appears to be an advanced nation in terms of welfare, with its four major social insurance plans, these systems are not yet mature and are not fulfilling their role as the primary safety net to counter social risks. The Government must, therefore, make improvements to the social insurance system that are consistent with Korea's socioeconomic conditions.

First, the range of insurance services must be extended and the amount of coverage must also continue to expand, to provide a certain degree of stability in the face of various social risks. Second, a balance must be struck between the levels of burdens and benefits in order to achieve not only overall financial stability, but also stability within the social insurance system. Third, there must be an overhaul in the management and operation of the social insurance system in order to enhance the system's efficiency and to raise the level of the system's convenience for welfare recipients.

While the need to reform the social insurance system

34

seems clear, a number of consequential problems are bound to emerge as a result of reform, such as the conflict of interest between different social groups. Rather than leaning towards the interests of any one particular social group, the Government will place priority on social integration and improvement in the welfare of the total population.

2.1. Old Age Pension

The Government expanded its national pension coverage to include the urban self-employed in April 1999, thereby introducing a more comprehensive pension system which provides greater security to a larger number of people in their old age. Under this new plan, a more equitable distribution of income among different income groups is expected, and Korea will be better prepared for the needs of an aging population through provisions of an improved old-age pension plan. Korea will, thus, truly be on its way towards becoming an advanced welfare society.

There are several difficulties, however, that must be overcome to effectively implement this plan for assuring a minimum level of social security for the aged. One problem, for example, is the low reported incomes of many self-employed persons that results in disproportionately low contribution levels. Although there has been a significant improvement in the accuracy of reporting of stated incomes since efforts were first made to identify professionals who have high incomes, further effort must be made to eliminate this problem.

Another similar problem is that approximately 5 million people are exempt from contribution payments. The majority of people who are exempt from contributions are individuals who have become unemployed or who have retired as a result of the economic crisis. A large number of exempt persons are thought to be workers who participate in some form of income-earning activity, but who have reported themselves to be exempt from contribution because they do not have the ability to pay contributions. The problem is that many of these people who now claim exemption from contributions will in the future be excluded from old-age pension coverage, because they did not make contribution payments.

As job opportunities for the partially unemployed have shrunk since the onset of the economic crisis, this problem could persist despite eventual economic recovery. In response to this problem, the national pension plan will in the year 2000 seek to protect the underprivileged by placing them in small businesses with less than four employees, thereby lessening their contribution burden.

Pension benefits will escalate as the number of people receiving pension benefits increases, as a result of: (1) relaxing the eligibility requirements of the unemployed in relation to pensions, for example early retirement, and disability and survivor pensions; and (2) expanding coverage to farmers and fishermen over the age of 60 who have contributed to the fund for more than five years.

An ancillary thrust toward refining the national pension system is to stabilize fund operations and to raise the level of professionalism and transparency in fund management. The structure of fund management has been reorganized and a specialist has been hired to raise efficiency. Greater participation in the implementation of the national pension plan, including fund management, by representatives of the contributors, will be made to ensure continuous improvements in Korea's old-age security system.

2.2. Health Insurance Against Various Diseases

Compared to other kinds of insurance, health insurance was introduced relatively early. Ten years have passed since the establishment of a nationwide health insurance plan. While health needs have been quantitatively satisfied, the system needs to be further refined, due to such problems as the low level of benefits relative to the high contribution rates.

According to a recent research report, the average contribution of health insurance patients was 59 percent of total treatment costs. Within that figure, the contribution rates for treatment by outpatients and by admitted patients were 66 percent and 44 percent, respectively. This rate of outpatients to admitted patients has been steadily increasing over the last few years. If contribution rates relative to the cost of treatment remain as high as they are now, health insurance will not fulfil its role as a social insurance system.

To reduce the cost of providing health benefits, the Government is seeking ways to improve the health insurance system in real terms, through amendments to the National Health Insurance Act and the subsequent integration of the health insurance system. The integrated management system for health insurance will aid social integration by improving income redistribution and risk dispersion and will enable a more efficient operation and management of health insurance.

The Government will further attempt to reduce healthcare costs by promoting a financial stabilization plan for comprehensive health insurance and will ensure the efficient use of the contributions from healthcare recipients. In the long term, the quality of health services will, therefore, improve and the burden on households in utilizing healthcare services will be reduced by transforming the current system from high-contributions, low-benefits to adequate contributions, adequate benefits.

2.3. Employment Insurance for all Workers

Employment insurance is being introduced as part of a

more aggressive employment policy that aims to provide stable opportunities for economic activity through the payment of unemployment benefits to the temporarily unemployed and to develop employment stability and job-capabilities of workers and the unemployed. The scope of coverage has rapidly expanded since the recent economic crisis and subsequent restructuring efforts. With the expansion of the program in October 1998 to all workplaces, employment insurance has come to play an important function as the primary social safety net for the temporarily unemployed.

Important issues for the future remain, however, such as the prevention of quantitative and qualitative problems of disbursing benefits and administering services, which may arise as coverage is expanded and the system continues to develop.

A mechanism is especially necessary to regulate workers who have relatively unstable employment. Although, employment assistance has been expanded to include part-time workers, a nationwide infrastructure to provide re-employment services is necessary. The management and operation of small workplaces must also be made more efficient, because the practical disbursement of benefits has been limited by a lack of adequate information, including information regarding true incomes.

Another knotty issue is the management of day laborers,

who are only required for short periods of time and are thus compelled to move from job to job. Their periods of employment are unpredictable and difficult to track. Plans to develop an employment management system specifically designed for day laborers is being formulated to resolve this issue.

The development of diverse, user-friendly programs and services to facilitate greater stability in employment and to enhance job capabilities will actively prevent further unemployment and increase the chances of reemployment. The range of benefits will be extended, while the level and periods of benefits will be rescheduled to better reflect the realities of unemployment and, thus, enhance the income security function of unemployment benefits.

2.4. Insurance Against Industrial Injury

Industrial accident insurance has the longest history of all the social insurance systems in Korea. Although many workers still do not work in a safe environment, industrial accident insurance does not yet cover all workers. These uncovered workers must be protected by expanding the coverage of industrial accident insurance and by improving the social security function. In pursuit of this end, coverage will be extended to all workplaces from July 2000, thereby protecting even workers employed by small businesses with less than four employees.

Under the same policy, a new system will allow small-business owners, who work alongside workers in the production process, to receive compensation in relation to damages suffered as a result of workplace accidents. The range of diseases and illnesses that are recognized as resulting from employment will be widened and the minimum living standards of survivors of industrial-accident victims will be ensured. Social equality will be aided by establishing equitable standards of maximum and minimum compensation where victims are involved in unstable forms of employment, such as part-time work, and benefits will be paid on the basis of the number of actual work days and income earned.

Until now, the emphasis has been on providing direct compensation to the injured worker. In the future, greater emphasis needs to be placed on job-rehabilitation programs, to enable the injured worker to reenter the workforce or otherwise find a job quickly. Hospitals for industrial accident victims must be established in each region, where there are professionals who can provide job-rehabilitation counseling, and where there are a variety of rehabilitation programs. Greater resources will be directed toward prevention programs, such as safety inspections and safety education, so as to preempt industrial accidents before they occur.

2.5. A More Efficient and Convenient Social Insurance System

The issue of the need for integrated management has recently been raised to further the efficiency, convenience, and equity of the social insurance system. The degree of efficiency in management and convenience to insured persons is currently very low, because there are separate, concurrent insurance schemes that serve a single needy recipient. For example, the eligibility criteria and income standards for contribution levies are different in each system and could thus lead to overlaps, which in turn, could mean greater inconvenience and burden to subscribers. The absence of an information network among the different systems prevents the sharing of information, thereby reducing the efficiency of information utilization.

To resolve these problems, the Tripartite Commission, composed of representatives from labor, management, and the Government, in February 1998, negotiated an integration plan for redefining contribution levies for employment insurance, industrial injury insurance, the national pension system, and health insurance. To formulate an integration strategy, the Social Security Council established the Planning Board for the integration of the four major insurance plans.

The new strategy proposes to integrate the specific types of insurance eligibility criteria, contribution levies, and the structure of management and operations. To assure the long-term development and convenience of the social system, integration of the insurance system will be based on the principles of efficiency, democracy, transparency, and professionalism.

3. Expansion of Social Welfare Services

The role of social welfare services is growing in importance in the face of the complex and manifold changes resulting from industrialization, urbanization, and the emergence of the Information Age. The need to provide a more elaborate and diverse social assistance system is, consequently, continually increasing, because of the increasing numbers of those who cannot fit into channels of mainstream employment.

The welfare needs of the socially underprivileged, including the disabled, the aged, women, and children are gaining in importance in modern, advanced countries. In response to these growing needs, there will be an expansion in the number of people who will be covered by the old-age pension plan and the amount of benefit payments will be raised each year to secure the incomes of the aged who are excluded from other public pension plans.

The Elderly Employment Center and Elderly Joint Workplaces will also be expanded to encourage the re-employment of the elderly. An active life for the aged will be ensured by increasing the range of local community volunteer activities and by providing greater assistance to service centers for the elderly, such as senior citizens' recreation centers and senior citizens' welfare centers.

Opportunities for participation in society must be facilitated through the development of various social participation programs and home-care. Welfare services must be expanded for the elderly who are ill and the efficiency of long-term admission facilities must be increased for the more seriously ill among the elderly, such as those with degenerative diseases. Also, the safety and independence of the elderly need to be guarded by providing support services through a health and welfare service network.

Social integration for disabled people needs to be achieved through the provision of greater equality in participation and opportunity. To attain integration, several actions must be taken. Facilities and rehabilitation assistance must be expanded to provide stability in the daily living of the low-income disabled and provide independence for the disabled who receive home-care. The Government will also review payment schedules for those on low incomes to better reflect their needs and will gradually increase payments. Beginning in the year 2000, coverage of national protection and assistance will be broadened by increasing the range of recognized disabilities, including chronic kidney and heart diseases, chronic mental illness, and autism. In the future, various service programs will continue to be developed in consideration of the changing characteristics and demands of the disabled.

Children are another class of the vulnerable in society and are also our future. Assistance must, therefore, be directed to create an environment in which children can grow in a safe and healthy way. Their right to life, growth, and development should be assured. Since the recent economic crisis, the number of children who are abused and are in need of protection has been increasing. Assistance must first and foremost be provided to children who are not being protected in the home or those who are being deprived of opportunities for healthy growth.

The Government will strengthen the protection of children's living standards, provide education assistance, and give greater support and protection to children who are heads of their households. Free childcare programs in rural areas for children under five years of age from low income families have been in effect since late 1999 and will be extended to the entire nation in the year 2000. While childcare assistance programs for children under five years of age will continue to be supported, education assistance will be provided to all middle and vocational high school students who run their own households to ensure that their basic needs are met.

The basic direction of women's welfare is to promote women's health, to improve their competitiveness, and to enhance women's rights and status by providing a wide range of services. The Government will concentrate its efforts on balancing maternal and child healthcare programs among regions and classes for the promotion of women's health. In addition, women's pension rights will be secured and assistance will be extended to single-mother households and to the female unemployed for improving women's competitiveness. Opportunities for participation in society by women will be increased through the provision of adult education programs that are especially designed for women.

The welfare service system needs to be augmented, both in terms of quality and quantity, to ensure a better quality of life and to meet the diverse needs of society. The Government will continue to reform the welfare service system by focusing on the local administration of services, the efficient and adequate operation of welfare facilities, and the improvement of labor conditions for social workers and other employees.

Chapter 5

Welfare Through Participation in the Production Process

The right to work is a basic human right. People do not, however, engage in the production process solely to earn a living. Not only does work provide a living, but also provides a lifestyle and a sense of self-worth derived from job satisfaction. Incessant domestic and international competition has, however, led to companies being forced to reduce labor costs while less competitive enterprises were driven out of business. This trend has aggravated the instability in employment. The accelerating pace of the technological revolution is also expected to reduce the quality of employment for less-skilled workers, alienating some workers from the production process. One of the core goals of productive welfare, as conceived by President Kim, is to enhance job satisfaction by increasing the number of available jobs, as well as by improving the quality of jobs, and thus improving lifestyles without ignoring the principles of competitiveness nor market economics.

The goal of increasing job satisfaction cannot be achieved solely through unilateral government efforts. Job satisfaction can only be realized when it is based upon participation and mutual cooperation among labor, management, the bodies representing them, and the Government, as well as civic groups.

1. Job Creation and Job Security Through Human Resources Development

Despite the recent decline in unemployment since the abrupt increase immediately following the financial crisis of 1997, the long-term unemployment problem will continue to exist among those who generally have more difficulty finding jobs, such as young adults, women, and the elderly. Diversification of the forms of employment will also continue, as the number of regular workers decreases while that of non-regular workers increases, "non-regular" workers being, for example, leased workers, temporary workers, or day laborers.

To address these problems, unemployment measures

need to perform several tasks. First, 2 million new jobs should be created by the year 2002. Second, to systematically address the problems that have emerged as a result of the nation's crisis-induced restructuring process, such as unemployment, poverty, and a worsening in the fairness of income distribution, the social safety net needs to be reordered. This can be accomplished by improving the employment insurance system and by adopting specially targeted legislation, such as the National Minimum Living Standards Act. Active labor market policies, *e.g.* improved job-placement and vocational training programs, need to be strengthened to resolve existing problems and to prevent possible future employment hazards.

1.1. Job Creation and Retention

The Kim Dae-jung Administration is working hard to create stable jobs to effectively deal with unemployment. Ongoing restructuring efforts are being pushed to enhance the competitiveness of domestic enterprises, as well as to foster small venture businesses and small- to medium-sized information-based businesses. If the goal of creating 2 million new jobs is attained by the year 2002, the unemployment rate would decrease to under 5 percent. To enable the process of job creation, regulations will be amended, infrastructure to assist start-up businesses will be constructed, and labor market flexibility will be improved through better labor — management cooperation.

Opportunities for women to enter the labor market will also be created. As female workers tend to be particularly more skilled in information-based industries, work categories should be developed to cater to the skills of women. To make a serious effort in offering greater opportunities for female workers to participate in economic activities, the Government needs to establish a program that will relieve the burden of childcare and household chores for women.

Maintaining existing employment opportunities is as important as creating new jobs. The employment retention program, a program designed to prevent unemployment, will be flexibly implemented according to particular economic and employment circumstances. Because smaller companies in Korea have traditionally had difficulty raising growth capital, programs specially tailored for small- to medium-sized companies should especially be developed.

1.2. Prevention of Unemployment and Promotion of Prompt Re-employment

For those having difficulty in finding new employment, the Government will support their prompt reentrance into the labor market by enhancing the employment insurance system. To this end, the number of eligible employment insurance recipients will be increased to 7.6 million, or 80 percent of total workers, and to 20 percent of the total number of unemployed by the year 2002.

The Government is also planning to strengthen its already active labor market policy. This will be done through the timely provision of employment information and implementation of job placement and vocational training programs, which will allow workers to obtain and develop the skills needed to get a desired job. A variety of employment services tailored to each unemployment category, such as the elderly, young adults, women, and the long-term unemployed, will be facilitated through the integration of employment statistics into one data base. The Labor Market Information (LMI) system will serve to provide information on job availability, job market prospects, vocational training, and trends in the labor market. Other employment services, such as Employment Security Centers and employment service personnel, will be increased to meet the standards required of member nations by the Organization for Economic Cooperation and Development (OECD) and to better cope with increasing employment service needs.

1.3. Workforce Development Tailored to Industry Demand

The primary direction of workforce development will focus on remodeling the vocational training system to more effectively meet the level of demand from various industries, such as the knowledge-based industries.

The first task is to develop the long- and medium-term workforce required for the emerging information society. Vocational training to fill new categories of jobs should focus on training workers for jobs in high value-added industries, which will give them access to high-paying jobs. Public vocational training institutions will be transformed to specifically train personnel needed in key industries, such as knowledge-based manufacturing industries, and personnel lacking competitiveness in the job market.

Also important is the development of training programs for the private sector where implemented programs meet the needs of both the unemployed and the employers. To meet the demands of employers, training programs centered on their needs will be promoted. Providing greater opportunities for the participation of the private sector in the process of establishing and implementing training policies are also being planned.

The performance of trainees at the end of their training will be assessed and analyzed through a database containing information about the trainees, their employment status after training, and other pertinent statistics. By creating a competitive environment through government-supported performance-based training programs, the quality of the training institutions will be enhanced. To induce a more structured framework to more efficiently increase the nation's investment in workforce development, a national certification system for human resource development and corporate accounting standards will be introduced.

To better respond to changes in the industrial structure, the currently in place National Skills Qualification System will be expanded to include qualifications for knowledge-based industries and special or general office-work services. The criteria and method of examination will parallel those employed by the private sector to identify qualified job candidates who can meet the labor needs of industry.

1.4. Equal Opportunities and Training

The most important consideration for the Government in providing a better vocational training system is to provide equal opportunities to less-privileged workers, such as the less-educated, the low-skilled, young adults, and women. In today's Information Age, those having better-quality knowledge and more advanced technical skills will have relatively more opportunities to develop their vocational ability, thereby widening the gap between the privileged and the under-privileged.

In-depth vocational counseling programs will be provided for the long-term unemployed and young adults.

Counseling these people would enable them to better utilize vocational training, participate in public-works projects, and find supplementary jobs for extra income. Currently, when a business owner provides training for workers, he or she can receive a subsidy from the Government. Because the end-users of these programs are the workers, the training should accommodate their needs. The funds for loans to these workers should be increased to serve more people, while government subsidies granted to company-administered training programs should also be expanded. To make training available to people who must work while they study, training leave should be a part of employee benefits.

For these training programs to be available to everyone, regardless of who employs them, small- and medium-sized companies that have limited resources for training their employees ought to receive assistance from the Government. To offer these training programs to the widest possible constituency and to reduce costs, innovative new teaching strategies that utilize computers and the Internet will be prioritized and supported by the Government.

2. Improving Employment Conditions: Reinforcement of Labor Welfare

2.1. Enhancing Labor Welfare

Two recent phenomena have influenced the reconsideration of labor welfare in Korea; the economic crisis of late 1997 and globalization. Both have highlighted the defects in present employment conditions and income distribution, which manifests itself as an increasing disparity between the rich and the poor. The implications of these phenomena call for better support for low-wage workers. In contrast to workers in larger companies, workers in smaller and less-profitable companies have relatively inferior working conditions and require a more comprehensive labor welfare support.

Labor welfare policy and its administration requires a general overhaul and an integration of its dispersed functions for coherent and consistent delivery of welfare services. For example, the proposed Workers' Labor Welfare Act is scheduled to replace the Labor Welfare for Workers in Small to Medium Companies Act and the Improvement of Employment Conditions and Employment Security Support Act. This process of integration will help to reinforce the foundations of welfare policy.

Under the proposed Workers' Labor Welfare Act, a consistent strategy will implement projects to support the daily lives of workers and their families. One of these projects is a housing program that subsidizes purchase or key-money loans and provides rental assistance. Another project is the minimum living standards program which provides for an academic allowance and reimbursement of medical and certain living expenses. Other support policies will be adopted to enable workers to accumulate wealth through various savings strategies, employee stock ownership plans, for example.

2.2. Improving Conditions of Work

Koreans are known for their long working hours. Although the average individual's working hours has decreased over the past 10 years, Korea still has one of the longest workweeks in the world. Reduction of working hours can improve an individual's productivity by increasing his or her leisure time, which will in turn improve the individual's creativity and enthusiasm. Shorter working hours can also contribute to the creation of jobs. On the other hand, there is also a strong argument that conditions in Korea do not yet warrant introduction of shorter working hours. Labor unions, management, and the Government should further discuss ways to gradually reduce the actual number of working hours per week.

New, higher standards for working conditions in the labor market need to be formulated. Among current labor-related protection measures, some are unrealistic or the implementation differs from their original purpose. Revising these measures, along with improving the collective rights of workers and labor-union bargaining power, is required not only to ease unnecessary restrictions but also to improve working conditions. The Kim Dae-jung Administration will earnestly seek ways to improve the current system in consultation with representatives from the labor unions and management.

2.3. Improving Protection for Underprivileged Workers

Those workers who especially need more systematic protection with regard to their working conditions are non-regular workers, particularly day laborers and low-income employees in small businesses. For these workers, laws that provide social insurance have yet to be established. Even if such structural measures were in place, actual protection in many cases would not be available because of limited administrative capabilities for monitoring employer labor practices and imprecise personnel procedures. According to data gathered by researchers, many small businesses do not have proper documents for wage payments and, in some cases, there are no employment records at all. Given these circumstances, government employment policies, such as the payment of unemployment benefits, placement services, and vocational training programs, would seem to have a very limited impact on these workers.

To remedy this problem, systematic data on these workers needs to be collected. The next task would be to seek ways of gradually expanding the Government's total structural protection measures, taking into consideration the Government budget and the funds available to sustain existing social insurance plans.

To further enhance the protection of underprivileged workers, government policy should strengthen the administration of labor policies, especially the administration of labor standards and the administration of welfare services, to facilitate the implementation of new or expanded services. If, however, these disadvantaged workers are included in the labor-welfare system, employers will have to shoulder some of the burden in the short term, which will increase their personnel costs. However, in the long run, this burden should eventually bear benefits for both corporate management and the national economy by enhancing the vocational ability of underprivileged workers.

3. Labor Participation and Industrial Democracy

3.1. Labor Participation in a Wide Range of Activities

Worker participation through trade unions is the very first step towards industrial democracy and one of the most fundamental channels of participation for laborers. It is important to establish channels for trade unions and their workers to participate in a wide array of activities, such as production procedures, workers' welfare, distribution of benefits, and industrial safety.

To survive in this era of increasing global competition, President Kim suggested in his essay, "The Direction of the Labor Movement in Korea" (Sasang-Gae, 1955), that Korean companies need to develop ways to encourage cooperation between labor and management and to increase worker participation. Companies will not be able to survive in the future if their businesses are not based on creativity and voluntary workplace involvement by their employees. In Mr. Kim's words:

> *While we should always respect private ownership and individual creativity, we should reject unilateral dominance by capital and seek a situation where labor, capital and technology cooperate with each other on an equal footing. By doing so, we will enable rapid improvement of productivity and ensure fair distribution of profits to workers and technicians.*

Although more than 40 years have passed since Mr. Kim first introduced the ideas of labor participation in welfare and industrial democracy, his ideas have   strong relevance today. In particular, the term "cooperationism," which he coined to suggest the direction of future labor—management relations, is worth noting even today.   Also, new labor issues, such as employment adjustment, overhauling salary scales, and continuing education are now arising.   In order to smoothly resolve these issues, employers should take the initiative of seeking ways to ensure worker participation.   To achieve this relationship, however, trust between labor and management is needed.   The surest way to build this trust is to initiate worker participation.

In building trust, we need to firmly establish practices that encourage worker participation in management and capital ownership, as well as to seek structural measures to support these practices.   In particular, worker participation in capital could bring about many positive results.   For employers, the employee stock ownership plan could function as a safety valve, ensuring managerial rights against unwanted merger and acquisition bids.   Employee ownership participation could also serve as a way to improve the financial performance of a company by reducing labor costs, such as wages.   For the workers, owning the company's equity would assuredly strengthen employee interest in the company and serve as an effective means to accumulate personal wealth, thus, bringing benefits to both the employers and the employees.

In times of full-scale restructuring, when the system of corporate governance is being radically transformed, expansion of worker participation would contribute to making the corporate governance system more sound. Moreover, by exercising shareholder rights through employee stock ownership, expansion of worker participation could contribute to the democratization of the company's decision-making process and would also provide a method of monitoring corporate management by workers. Worker participation and the wealth accumulation programs for workers could become a very positive policy package.

There are many ways to increase worker participation in the decision-making process. Sharing corporate management information, having representation on corporate boards, and continually participating in the Labor — Management Council, a consultative body at the workplace level, are a few ways that should be sought. Since the Labor — Management Council of the Tripartite Commission is already a statutory body, it could become an effective vehicle for worker participation. Because the failure to disclose management and accounting information to workers has been one of the main factors that contributed to the creation of mistrust between labor and management, sharing corporate management information could serve as the simplest way to build mutual trust and strengthen cooperation between labor and management.

3.2. Tripartite Cooperation

In overcoming the economic crisis, it became evident that new insight into employment and unemployment issues was necessary to survive in today's highly competitive open market. Unemployment is not just a problem for the Government and the unemployed, it is the mutual responsibility of all citizens. To sustain jobs, not only is government support needed, but maximum effort from both employers and workers are simultaneously required.

Labor, management, and the Government should co-operate to stabilize employment, create jobs, support the basic needs of the unemployed, and assist the temporarily unemployed in finding new jobs. The Government will also strive to decrease unemployment through job-creation policies. The Government's present unemployment measures will focus more on the mid- to long-term outlook, as the immediate unemployment crisis has been somewhat curbed. The Government will continue to support lifelong education to cope with the new vocational demands of the constantly changing business environment. In line with the Government's efforts, labor and management should take further steps to cooperate and maintain employment.

With regard to employment policies, the role of trade unions should be extended. In particular, the continuation of training and education, which in most cases increases worker productivity, should not be left just to employers. Training would be more effective if it were conducted with the cooperation of both labor and management. With the advent of knowledge-based industries, this could become an important element of assuring job security, increasing wages, and expanding trade-union membership by providing more services that would attract new members.

Labor involvement in formulating unemployment support services, such as job-placement services, should be strengthened. The Government, in a bid to achieve this goal, will actively seek ways to entrust responsible and competent trade unions to operate some of the unemployment-prevention projects. By doing so, the labor—management relationship, which currently focuses on benefits distribution and wage bargaining, could be developed into a relationship that includes the development of human resources. This modification of focus will alter the development of the Government-led unemployment prevention and welfare systems into a partnership between the Government and the private sector.

3.3. The Role of the Tripartite Commission

The ideal labor–management relationship would be democratic and productive in which labor and management solve problems through dialog as equal partners. An accurate understanding of the labor–management relationship by the three parties of labor, management, and the Government is, however, vital. Equally important is that they build mutual trust based upon an accurate understanding of each other.

One step in the direction of dialog in the content of mutual trust is the Tripartite Commission, a consultative body at the national level which consists of representatives from labor, management, and the Government. The Tripartite Commission is currently in the process of reshaping the labor–management relationship, which is needed amid the wave of corporate restructuring now underway in Korea. Achieving structural reform will, however, not be easy. Cooperation between labor and management needs to grow through improved policies and further political dialog. Efforts should also be made to implement labor and structural reform within the framework of the Tripartite Commission, where one would expect that a partnership based upon trust between labor, management, and the Government will be formed.

Chapter 6

Welfare for the Self-Support of the Underprivileged

All households below the poverty line will be provided with assistance to achieve minimum living standards, regardless of the individual's ability to work, by October 2000 with the proposed implementation of the National Minimum Living Standards Act. There are still insufficiencies in the budget, however, and the system needs further improvements, but the framework for a public assistance program will be created. A good national welfare system cannot be a substitute for feelings of self-esteem and worth that stem from employment and independence. Most unemployed and homeless people desire stable jobs rather than financial assistance or participation in public works. Labeling unemployed people, as having no capability or no will to work, undermines their desire for self-sufficiency, independence, and work. A pragmatic welfare system, along with aggressive policies, is necessary to provide jobs, so that these individuals can become self-supporting and achieve independence.

1. Protection Based on Social Integration

In the current labor market, finding a job is quite difficult for less educated, low-skilled, middle-aged, and long-term unemployed people. While the number of jobs in the rapidly changing technology sector is rising, jobs in the traditional industries are decreasing. Middle-aged laborers, for whom adjustment to the new industrial structure is difficult, are at a high risk of unemployment and of being permanently excluded from the labor market. During the high-growth and low-unemployment period of the 1970s, self-support was attainable through one's sheer will and effort, but now a low-growth and high-unemployment environment is fast approaching, thus, making self-support difficult to achieve. Meanwhile, the despair of the long-term unemployed has deepened, and is exacerbated by the inability of the family to act as the primary social safety net.

1.1. Instituting Social Integration

Long-term unemployment remains an unresolved issue,

even in advanced nations with adequate welfare. The unemployment rate in Europe has remained at approximately 10 percent for close to 20 years. Traditional welfare expansion, however, has reached its financial limit and market-oriented solutions have failed to have a positive effect on job creation and the elimination of poverty. This is one reason that the "third way," or a social enterprise policy, has appeared in European countries since the latter half of the 1980s. Under this policy, alienation and poverty are not left to be resolved by the Government or the market, but rather, by the regional communities.

Examples of European attempts to find a remedy to chronic long-term unemployment abound. In the United Kingdom, the New Deal policy enables people who have been unemployed for a long period of time to derive some satisfaction by doing volunteer work. France strengthened its policies for the long-term unemployed and homeless in July 1998 with passage of the Alienation Prevention and Withdrawal Act. In Italy, where the unemployment rate reached 12 percent in the late 1980s, a collaborative social system was legislated in 1991 with the Government supporting private-sector job-creation programs for the long-term unemployed.

A common element among these welfare systems is that they provide payments to the unemployed so that they can sustain minimal living standards. Another common element in Europe's approach to unemployment is adoption of locally centered job-creation policies where local civic groups administer various assistance programs. Many of these countries are continuing to make efforts to create jobs through programs, such as minimum living standard assistance for senior citizens living alone, after-school tutoring programs for low-income children, financial assistance for cultural and recreational activities in each region, natural disaster restoration, and the hiring of school-safety personnel.

1.2. Self-Support as Welfare

Assisting an individual to become autonomous is not an evasion of responsibility by the Government, but rather, cultivates human potential, creates a sense of stability, and generates productivity. Assistance includes motivating people to find the will to work again if it has already been lost, which is the reason that rehabilitation programs such as psychological counseling are conducted in self-help programs.

Positive welfare programs to encourage self-support correspond to the needs of the underprivileged and take the third way approach, which utilizes community resources as well as public funds. The third way has a comprehensive welfare program that ranges from counseling to job-training facilities and extending start-up loans. This system involves active participation from communities, religious organizations, citizens' groups, and labor unions.

2. Expansion of Third Way Type Self-Help Programs

Assistance to aid individual self-support is a new idea in Korea. Assistance which includes job training, job assistance, loan programs for the unemployed, and public works projects can be called both a labor-linked welfare policy and a program to assist self-support.

The proposed National Minimum Living Standards Act regulates self-help associations and other programs that promote self-support. When necessary, provisions of the act will offer financial support to individuals so that he or she can purchase products or rent public land. Minimum living standards will be guaranteed to any individual having the ability to work.

Protection of minimum living standards and labor-linked programs are not yet in effect. Job training and job assistance are still not unified and management guidance for loans to maintain a minimum standard of living have not yet been formally proposed. Assistance programs for self-support are still inadequate because of the lack of awareness of self-help programs in rural areas. People who need minimum living standard loans are giving up their efforts to attain them because they do not have the necessary collateral or a personal guarantor.

2.1. People-Oriented Welfare

There is a limit to the support provided by the official welfare system for the underprivileged. Self-support is impossible to achieve merely by providing information alone. Before applying for minimum living standards assistance, evidence of the individual's dire circumstances is needed. This is why a people-friendly welfare system is necessary to provide services in geographic areas where the underprivileged are concentrated.

The Government will considerably expand the 20 existing self-help assistance centers across the nation. Social welfare centers, churches, and other nationwide organizations will take control of the assistance centers. These self-help centers will be able to act as a one-stop service center, providing counseling, job training, job assistance, public works opportunities, and assistance to start up new businesses. Separate information centers will be established in the large cities and provinces to assist small-scale self-help centers. These facilities will be responsible for providing an information exchange among larger self-help assistance centers, for educating workers, and for cooperating with local authorities.

The creation of new jobs in the public sector is also

necessary. Employment should be continuously created by focusing on public works programs that have proven to be successful, such as visiting nurse services for the needy and the less mobile, welfare assistants, and forest cultivation and waste management staffers. Some of these programs could be implemented by the private sector while the public works programs are being implemented by the Government.

2.2. Community Self-Support Assistance Fund

The Self-support Assistance Fund is made up of community money necessary to assist underprivileged individuals who find it impossible to start up businesses through the existing public funding system. This system, which is already being expanded in the European countries, is a measure to prevent the long-term unemployed or low-income individuals from experiencing setbacks for not having the necessary collateral or personal guarantors.

There are, in fact, many self-help funds being managed and operated in European countries, *e.g.* Banca Etica in Italy and Afile-77 in France. Most of these are established at the local-authority level in large cities and are composed of central-government funds, regional self-support fund contributions, donations from civic groups, religious organizations, private enterprises, and from citizens in the general population. These services provide loans to long-term unemployed persons wishing to start a business. The feasibility of the business, possibilities for stable job creation, and profitability are all taken into consideration in the credit review process. If a loan is provided, it is supported from the internal fund, and if the loan is large, then a guarantor stands for the bank. If the enterprise is not feasible, or if there is a lack of skills or business experience, then a new enterprise is recommended or training is suggested.

Although the establishment and operation of the private and public cooperative fund will not be easy in Korea, the Government along with private organizations will search for a multifaceted assistance policy. The self-support program will not be a program based on waiting, but will be a program based on movement. The program envisioned for Korea will be a combination of general assistance programs and specialized assistance programs that cater specifically to each individual. To make these programs successful, there must be cooperation between the public welfare system and the private sector. For these reasons, the private sector, social welfare centers, and religious organizations, which have been active in assisting the poor, are expected to play a pivotal role. Third way type assistance to promote self-support will become a new welfare model for the year 2000.

3. Strengthened Cooperation Between the Public and Private Sector

3.1. Administrative Assistance for Self-Help Programs

The foundation of productive welfare will be laid by providing opportunities to experience the satisfaction and joy of work. To achieve the goals of productive welfare, the Government has affirmed the importance of self-support programs by already having included these programs in unemployment and welfare measures. The self-support assistance centers are also being expanded and the implementation of other self-support programs is also being considered as a countermeasure to unemployment. Reform is also being sought to enable the temporary public labor program to be implemented with the vision of implementing third way type programs. Efforts are also being made to prepare a system and policy foundation for the self-help fund. Private-sector activities are being supported and legislation will be proposed to encourage a cooperative association between the public and private sectors.

Information centers are being operated to assist self-help programs in both the big cities and in the provinces, while regional self-help assistance funds are being supported. Local authorities generally develop active programs that often include providing space for self-help associations and job-assistance services. They also have the responsibility of developing models for education, both public and private. Overseas examples show that cooperation is necessary to gain fruitful results from self-support programs.

Various jurisdictional rights will be entrusted to local authorities to administer social self-support programs. The current system of allocating welfare funds to local government authorities will be reviewed with a view toward allocating subsidy payments according to regional needs. In this way, social self-support will be closely linked to social welfare and employment services.

3.2. Private Sector-Led Self-Support Development

Total responsibility for the implementation of third way type programs by the private sector would not only better promote the self-help program, but would generally be more efficient in overseeing the establishment of the self-help assistance fund, counseling, education, and job-training pro-grams.

The function of citizens' groups, which formerly worked for the protection of people's rights in poor communities, must be newly established by linking people who need help to local resources. Religious organizations are particularly active in providing various welfare services for the needy in their neighborhoods. The Government encourages these local efforts and intends to continue to support existing programs while implementing new programs for the economic independence of the underprivileged. Community welfare centers will be very effective if self-support programs are managed with the wisdom accumulated from experience; thus, facile communications and the free exchange of information among the nation's network of service agencies will be encouraged.

Enterprises and labor unions can also play an important role in helping unemployed laborers to become self-supporting. Labor unions can manage self-help assistance centers to provide self-support opportunities to retirees who have caught acute diseases or who suffer from chronic debilitation. Enterprises can help to generate local economic activity by purchasing products produced by self-help associations or by providing jobs.

Self-support means the ability to support oneself. Aid from the community is, however, a necessary condition to allow many underprivileged people to live independently. For these reasons, participation and support of the community are necessary.

Chapter 7

Welfare for
a Better Quality of Life

Social policies need to remove any discrimination against people who suffer from deprivation and a lack of basic human necessities. Policies should move towards creating a society that secures economic prosperity for the present generation, while ensuring social progress for future generations.

In recognizing the importance of social policies, President Kim's Administration is committed to continuously addressing problems in the areas of education, health, culture, and the environment, which are considered important for a higher quality of life.

1. Equal and Lifelong Education

In order to put the fundamental principle of "productive

welfare" into action, each individual should be given equal access to education, which, in turn, requires a social infrastructure in which each individual can enjoy lifelong educational opportunities. Lifelong education is the means to the end in the implementation of our national policy, which is aimed at promoting productivity and a better quality of life across the entire spectrum of society.

1.1. Equality in Education

Education should focus on building a society where individuals with different personalities and competency levels respect and cooperate with one another to promote mutual prosperity and to nourish creativity. Equitable educational opportunities for all citizens will enable individuals to easily adapt to the emerging information-based society.

Although our education system seeks "to produce well-rounded individuals," in reality, more emphasis has been placed on developing analytical skills and stretching mental capabilities rather than promoting creativity. In evaluating scholastic performance, disproportionately higher priority has been given to student test results and grades than to student progress and the degree of their endeavors.

The established formal education system has failed to carry out its intended functions. Education's failure is visible in the increase in social tension, as many parents are forced to pay for the high cost of private tuition. Those families who cannot afford to provide supplementary schooling must contend with disadvantages suffered by their children. Children of low-income families receive fewer educational opportunities and are highly likely to become marginalized in their formal schooling. This growing handicap of children from lower-income families intensifies the need for reform in the present education system.

The Government will place more efforts on securing equality in educational opportunity so that no one will be disadvantaged because of economic reasons. To attain equal educational opportunity, the Government will increase financial assistance to low-income families in the form of low-interest student loans. From the year 2000, tuition for middle- and high-school students in low-income families will be covered by government subsidies. Consequently, disadvantaged families will be able to receive free schooling. School meals will also be provided free-of-charge for students from low-income families.

With regard to pre-school education, which is dominated by private institutions, the current subsidies given to low-income families, primarily in farming or fishing communities, will be scaled up by the year 2002. Schools and educational programs will be created or reinforced to cater specifically to at-risk students, including those who have left school or students with mental or physical disabilities. The Government will concentrate on reforming education by promoting "educational welfare," in order to decrease expenses paid for private tuition.

1.2. Lifelong Education

Lifelong learning not only helps individuals to realize their goals and increase employment flexibility, but also contributes to developing a highly creative society. The establishment of a lifelong learning system can develop a strong relationship between jobs and education in order to cultivate greater productivity. The existing education system does not offer a systematic link between education and employment. Similarly, the time, energy, and finances spent on education may seem ineffective and inefficient both to the individual and to the society where there are job shortages in the labor market.

The coming new millennium will bring forth a knowledge-based society, where creativity will become one of the major determinants of an individual's quality of life and the level of national competitiveness. In preparation for an era that will demand new levels of knowledge and information, the Government will attempt to create continuing educational opportunities that are available to everyone. This will be a challenge, as Korea does not have a well-developed lifelong education system.

With the goal of establishing a lifelong education system, the Government will lay the foundation for "a society of open education and lifelong learning." In August 1999, the Social Education Act was replaced by a new Lifelong Education Act. Over the coming years, the law will allow individuals to continue their education through avenues, such as part-time enrollment in schools, university courses offered through the Internet, and recognition of qualifications received at industrial-site colleges. In addition, a rotational education system will be established for those who desire to pursue training in a field different from their present area of specialty. These adults will be able to receive university education, even after being employed by a company.

The Framework Plan for the Comprehensive Education of the Elderly is an extension of lifelong education, or continuing education. The plan for the elderly will be devised and implemented to aid the growing number of senior citizens who strive to be economically self-supporting and to make a positive contribution to society.

To increase the efficiency and effectiveness of vocational and educational training, the Government intends to organize the Framework Plan for Vocational Education and Training. This law will link education to the labor market by restructuring vocational education in high schools so that workers can acquire new technical skills, even after graduation. Specialized high schools and junior colleges will be fostered and various departments at technical universities will be reorganized to maximize the services and training that are offered and are unique to the respective schools. All these advances are aimed solely at ensuring that every individual has the opportunity to continue their education throughout their lives. When a system of lifelong education is firmly established, no individual in the nation will be denied the opportunity to obtain education because of a lack of money.

2. Establishment of a Lifelong Health Maintenance System

The notion that the right to good health is a basic human right has become widely accepted. Providing health services is, thus, a responsibility of government and is specified in the Korean Constitution: *i.e.* "The health of all citizens shall be protected by the State." (Article 36, Paragraph 3)

Till now, the role of the Government in public health has remained rudimentary. The Government has overlooked the importance of establishing the infrastructure and the various programs necessary to improve public health. In Korea, the healthcare system has depended largely on the private sector for its services, while the role of the Government has been minimal.

Through the private sector, the quality of public health-care improved substantially, generally meeting the public's healthcare needs. The private sector, however, has focused most of its energy on simply treating diseases and has failed to tackle newly emerging demands in healthcare for preventing disease.

Diseases that are most threatening to society have evolved from acute to chronic status and are commonly associated with unhealthy lifestyles. Another changing element in healthcare is the rising number of elderly people in the population; the percentage of senior citizens has been projected to be 14 percent of the total population by the year 2020. These pathologic and demographic changes in the healthcare equation indicate a dramatic increase in the need for long-term healthcare that includes rehabilitation, medical services, and hospice services.

The proper funding and effective management of healthcare services will, thus, be an area of focus for the Government in the near future. These shifting trends require an assortment of different strategies in the healthcare system that will require new methods for delivering and maintaining healthcare services.

2.1. Treatment Versus Lifelong Health

The current healthcare system, which focuses on the

treatment of diseases, should be extended to include lifelong health, attacking such issues as disease prevention, good health education, and lifelong health management. This new paradigm of healthcare will be pursued so that individuals can receive proper healthcare from prenatal development to old age.

The Government will also formulate comprehensive healthcare programs to cater specifically to senior citizens and the disabled. To achieve this goal, the Government will tap into public resources and extend incentives to the private sector to encourage their involvement in healthcare reform.

2.2. Improved Healthcare

To improve healthcare, the Government will develop and maintain new healthcare services, such as long-term care, home care, and community healthcare services, along with hospices and rehabilitation centers. The Government will play a vital role in implementing these services. As seen in the United States and Japan, the private healthcare sector within a competitive market cannot fully support healthcare services alone. A more active role for the Government will, therefore, be introduced. Intervention by the Government does not, however, necessarily reduce the role of the private sector. While the Government is responsible for the planning, implementation, evaluation, and monitoring of healthcare programs, healthcare services should be delivered in partnership with the private sector.

2.3. Efficient Healthcare

To develop efficient healthcare, the Government will develop a clear direction for healthcare services and introduce an innovative payment system, as well as an effective administrative system. Active participation by the private sector will also be encouraged. To provide better healthcare services, the specific needs of communities will also be addressed. In the next century, with rising incomes and growing demands for better healthcare, a sophisticated healthcare industry will be needed. The Government, therefore, plans to develop the healthcare industry into one of the core industries of the nation's future economy. While improving domestic healthcare, these efforts should strengthen Korea's competitiveness in the global market and provide a better quality of life. To achieve these goals, a revision of healthcare law, effective administration, establishment of a medical history information network, and sufficient investments in the healthcare sector is essential.

The Government's role in public healthcare will, thus, become more important in the near future. In the new era of the 21st Century, economic development will take place along with an effective healthcare system. As experienced by some   countries, poor public health management can become a great burden to the nation. Increasing healthcare expenditures can cause a financial crisis and disrupt sound economic development. Consequently, establishing efficient lifelong healthcare can nourish the quality of life and stimulate further social development.

3. Augmentation of Cultural and Leisure Lifestyles

3.1. Elevating Cultural Aspirations

The criteria for judging the quality of life are changing as Korea's economic growth continues and personal incomes rise. The majority of people are enjoying a life that is not only materially satisfying, but is also textured with cultural and leisure satisfaction. Culture and leisure are no longer enjoyed exclusively by the privileged classes, but have become a basic part of most people's lives.

President Kim Dae-jung emphasized that, "it is no longer a world where human beings pursue happiness by solving the problem of securing their food, clothing, and shelter. Improvement of culture, leisure, sports, *etc.*, is also necessary for improving the quality of life." Another factor that is also helping to improve lifestyles and is becoming increasingly more significant in modern

Korea is the gradual reduction in working hours, which in turn, extends the amount of time available for leisure-time activities. More leisure time further affects society by altering production and demand. New products and new services will fuel further economic expansion and will spur creativity in all aspects of productive life.

The importance of Korea's change in priorities from overcoming poverty to the demand for an enhanced lifestyle connotes the future of Korean society. Appropriate and carefully considered government policies can serve to nurture this process of social development.

3.2. Expansion of Cultural Facilities and Improvement of Management Methods

In accordance with the increasing national interest and participation in cultural and leisure activities, new or expanded cultural services are in demand. Facilities where people can easily have access to culture and art, such as museums, art galleries, and public libraries, must be augmented. The multifaceted cultural appetite of citizens in local communities must be satisfied by constructing and operating auditoriums for public performances, topic-specific libraries, cultural-heritage museums, and other kinds of facilities that display unique regional attributes.

Cultural welfare must be extended to embrace citizens of all ages. Large cities, such as Seoul, are often the focal points for cultural activities. To make cultural experiences available to nearly everyone in the population, cultural resources must proliferate everywhere in the country. The Administration has plans to expand cultural tour programs by organizing regional tours that highlight the uniqueness and creativity of Korea's various geographic regions. Kyungju, for example, is often referred to as the "Museum without Walls," because of the region's opulent preservation of historical sites. Well-organized tour programs can appeal to both native Koreans and foreign tourists, as well as to scholars.

If culture is to truly become a part of individual lifestyles, then cultural pursuits should be made available to people of all ages. Young children have different cultural needs than do adults. Consequently, cultural activities that help children enjoy, discover, and develop their individual talents must be tailored toward developing a lifelong sense of cultural values. Some of the cultural activities that appeal to the needs of children include hands-on zoos where children can touch the animals, and summer camps in the countryside that specialize in art, music, science, or handicrafts in relaxed settings that encourages self-exploration and creativity.

With many households now having two wage earners, often by choice rather than by necessity, the family has less opportunity to spend time together. The debate about the relative importance of the quantity or the quality of time spent together as a family may continue to rage among family scholars, but any kind of shared time in the pursuit of constructive leisure can be considered "good" time by any standard of measurement.

Creating family-oriented community centers that provide a wide range of services from athletic facilities to community training and information assistance, is a step toward developing community centered family leisure resources. These facilities can be staffed by local volunteers, which not only reduces the cost of implementation, but also encourages a broad base of community involvement. Picnic grounds, overnight camping sites, guided scenic tours, and facilities for boating, swimming, skiing, and mountain trekking represent additional opportunities for productive leisure that can be enjoyed by the whole family.

To fulfill this aspiration of dispersing cultural opportunities throughout the nation, youth training centers will be put into service in cities and counties around the country. Along with the expansion of these local facilities, the decentralization of these services will be made by shifting administrative and fiscal control from the national government to the respective local governments. The objective is to encourage the efficient implementation of services that are responsive to the needs of the people. Local fiscal responsibility will also encourage a more disciplined and responsible use of available funding, thus leading to efficiently delivered services.

The central government can help local governments by expanding new information technologies which can easily deliver information services into homes via cable television and the Internet. An important element of local administration is the ability of local autonomous governing bodies to mobilize the good will of local residents, civic organizations, and religious groups to provide volunteer staffing of many of these welfare services. Many people who have achieved a high level of self-support would be honored to have an opportunity to return their good fortune to society by helping others in well-organized, well-managed, and disciplined volunteer programs that, in the long run, help everyone in society to live a better life.

3.3. Expansion of National Athletic Facilities and Local Tourism

Fostering a healthy lifestyle and enjoyable leisure time requires public facilities. Assistance will be offered to local communities for providing sports classes, building swimming pools, erecting stadiums, installing gymnasiums, and establishing sports clubs in every city and county. Such facilities provide for a variety of human needs, while giving families an opportunity to share some activities together, thus, enriching the nation's state of cultural welfare. The central government can leverage its own fiscal and administrative resources by offering tax incentives to the private sector and by licensing local entrepreneurs to operate government-owned facilities.

3.4. Cultural Participation for Alienated Regions and People

One legacy of Korea's past high-growth at-any-cost policy is the unequal geographic distribution of development. Certain areas of the country were favored over others, which tended to fuel regional friction and political confrontation. One of the major thrusts of the Kim Dae-jung Administration has been to resolve the inequitable distribution of wealth that has arisen across regional boundaries in Korea. The objective is to have all Koreans enjoy an equitable standard of living, regardless of where they live.

Social alienation for many women, for the disabled, for the less skilled and less educated, and for troubled youths, has for far too long been accepted by Korean society. The time has come for all people in the nation to be treated with fairness and given equal opportunities for education, jobs, lifestyle assistance, and the means to become self-supporting, according to the best of their abilities.

For those who cannot be fully integrated into the mainstream of productive activities through no fault of their own, public assistance will be administered under the principles of productive welfare, which assures a minimum standard of living while providing the means to participate in productive activities. The less educated can be trained at local community centers to fill jobs in local companies. Everyone should have the opportunity to enjoy a minimum standard of productive living.

Special attention should be given to troubled youths. Problems of the young, if not resolved, will re-emerge in the future in the form of high rates of crime, un-employment, and social dysfunction. Money well-spent for helping troubled youths offers society a high rate of investment return in terms of preventing unsolvable adult problems by attending to the solvable problems of the young.

The special burdens of homemaking and childcare that have been traditionally delegated to women must be re-ordered to accommodate society's need for the special talents that women often possess. The mushrooming information industry is an especially important pathway for the equitable participation of women in productive society, because many women are better prepared for jobs in the information industry than are men. To help women become participants in economic productivity, facilities that provide childcare and preschool education can provide a wonderland for children to develop academically, socially, and physically while giving women the opportunity to contribute their talents to a society that needs every person to contribute his or her unique individual talents in a highly competitive global village of commerce and international social life.

4. Building a Healthy Environment

4.1. Nature as the Origin of Life

In modern industrial society, where nature has become an object for exploitation, there is little harmony between human beings and nature. Consequently, over-exploitation of natural resources and environmental degradation have been prevalent problems all over the world today. Today's environmental problems are a threat to our existence and also to human dignity.

One way to overcome the threat to environment is to educate individuals on the fundamental relationship between nature and human beings. Not only does the vital relationship need to be recognized, but responsibility should be taken for the worsening of environmental problems. The consequences of careless behavior should be considered, because indifference to nature will deprive the next generation of the right to live in a clean environment. The vague notion that scientific developments will help to identify and resolve a diverse array of environmental problems must be abandoned.

As a necessary step, we should establish an entirely new social value system that regards nature, not as an object of exploitation, but rather as a source of life. Environmental welfare will guarantee present and future generations the right to live in a healthy environment.

4.2. The Environment and Industrial Competitiveness

People have a basic right to live in a clean environment. The Government, therefore, has the responsibility to guarantee a clean environment, because clean air and clean water are core conditions for the building of a healthy nation. Rapid urbanization and industrialization, as well as economic development in Korea, have, however, contributed to deepening environmental problems.

In the process of economic development, the lack of environmental awareness has led to an increase in pollution, which is now threatening our health. Environmental problems have even extended into conflicts in international trade. Industrial competitiveness is now even affected by long-term factors, such as developing new green technologies and processes.

We are also entering into a new era of international trade where trading in commodities and services must be compliant with international environmental standards and regulations. Every country should make their best effort to reduce emissions of greenhouse gases. The use of environmentally detrimental materials, such as ozone-layer depleting substances, are not allowed to use for production.

Under these circumstances, if a company tries to avoid compliance with environmental regulations, the company may risk its own survival in the world market. Without securing environmental competitiveness, Korea will fall behind in achieving a better quality of life and a higher level of industrial competitiveness. A new policy paradigm is, thus, required to comprehensively tackle environmental problems, as well as to address the relationship between the environment and the economy.

A new environmental policy paradigm should center on sustainable development that will enhance the effectiveness of environmental policy and on Korea's industrial competitiveness. A new environmental policy should be promoted through economic incentives and political persuasion. The path of the new policy should be to pursue practical environmental policies in conjunction with central and local governments, along with participation of the private sector.

4.3. From Aftercare to Prevention: The Transformation of Environmental Policy

The Government will make every effort to build environmentally sound living conditions so that individuals can enjoy a better quality of life. To achieve this goal, President Kim will shift the direction of his initiatives from regulation-oriented to prevention-oriented policies. Several changes in the existing set of regulations will redirect the focus of current environment management: ineffective regulations will be lifted; voluntary participation by businesses will be promoted; and economic incentives will be extended.

To make the future national land planning and economic development more environmentally friendly, a preliminary decision-making system will be established to strengthen the process of reviewing and assessing environmental performance. The Government will safeguard national health and natural ecosystems from environmental accidents caused by toxic chemicals and wastes, which are newly emerging as the nation's economic activity continues to expand and economic conditions change.

To create an environmentally friendly production pattern for industry, cleaner production systems and advanced environmental technology will be developed. Required new technologies include modifying production processes that emit high levels of pollutants, designing environmentally friendly products, and finding substitutes for harmful raw materials. The environmental industry, catering to environmental needs, will be nurtured as a strategic industry in the 21st Century. To encourage the development of the environmental industry, small- and medium-sized enterprises will be granted substantial support from the Government.

As consumers become increasingly aware of the environmental implications of a rise in living standards, the efforts to promote sustainable consumption, such as stimulating the Korean Eco-Labelling System and environmental charges, will be strengthened. To facilitate the free flow among interested parties of information on environmental industries and green products, an information exchange network will be established to share information both domestically and internationally.

There will also be a great effort to enhance environmental management techniques and environmental preservation policies at the local government level. Some of the policies will support environmentally friendly development programs and extend financial support to local governments. Furthermore, local governments will implement the Amenity Plan, which will attempt to make a pleasant and amenable living environment. The plan is to create a harmonious relationship between an individual and his or her natural surroundings. One way to achieve this is through active participation by local governments and by the residents of the community.

In order to address global environmental problems, the international environmental cooperation system needs to be strengthened. National efforts to cope with global environmental issues should also be systematized by establishing a national committee, which will provide a platform to hold international debates and an opportunity to integrate and adjust national policies with regard to global environmental issues.

Further efforts are needed to enhance the public's understanding of environmental policies. Information on environmental pollution and policies will be readily available to the public so they can voluntarily participate in rectifying some of the problems.

Part III

Expansion of Welfare Funding and Participatory Welfare

The most important issue for the implementation of productive welfare is to allocate adequate resources to assure the fulfillment of any legitimate demand for services. If any resources are limited, there will surely be disillusionment among the people. To avoid failure, the absolute amount of funding must be expanded and every effort must be made to utilize resources for the most efficient delivery of services. The tax base must be broadened in a fair and equitable manner for equitable income redistribution to successfully reach its goals. An equitable system of taxation and redistribution assures that all socioeconomic classes participate in the process of productive welfare. Comprehensive policy issues that enrich people's lives include education, healthcare, culture, environment, finance, and taxation. Also relevant are policies that create a welfare system which enables the Government, civic organizations, and citizens to actively participate in the attainment of a productive welfare society.

Chapter 8

Expansion of Welfare Budget and Tax Justice

1. Expansion of Welfare Budget

1.1. The Expansion of Welfare: A Timely Proposal

Democracy and economic growth have enabled developed countries to cultivate a high standard of living. The more comprehensive social security systems in some countries, however, threatened to bring about welfare states that weakened economies with chronic deficits caused by government over-spending. Since the 1980s, efforts have been made to strike a balance between efficient growth and equitable distribution of wealth. The challenge for us in Korea is to minimize the level of social welfare spending while maximizing benefits on the basis of sound funding.

Korea's social welfare budget as a percentage of total government expenditures is significantly less than most developed countries. Not only has the low level of expenditures constrained the expansion and improvement of the social welfare system, it has also indicated to the international community that the Government has not been committed to improving the quality of life of its citizens. Although the reorganization of the four social insurance systems and contributions from the private sector have rapidly increased the welfare budget in recent years, the total budget is still low in comparison to the budgets of other developed countries.

The Government, in recognizing the importance of expanding the welfare budget, planned to increase the percentage of total government spending on social welfare. The recent debt crisis, however, forced the Government to divert most available funds to shoulder the cost of financial restructuring, thereby temporarily limiting any increases in the welfare budget.

As the financial crisis dissipates, the Government does intend to expand the welfare budget by increasing the level of priority given to welfare policy. Funds will also be secured through the gradual expansion of the tax base. By improving tax administration to increase tax compliance, the Government can expand the social welfare fund without unfairly burdening low-income citizens.

1.2. Plans for the Efficient Operation and Execution of the Social Welfare System

To expand and increase the effectiveness of Korea's welfare system, the welfare budget must be enlarged and the available funds must be efficiently applied. The different welfare authorities need to be organized according to their areas of responsibility to maximize efficiency in the use of available, and perhaps limited, welfare funds. For the various social insurance programs, benefits will be tied to liability to ensure efficient expenditures. The primary focus of President Kim's Administration is to increase the budget for public support of welfare services for the poor.

Along with making the distribution of welfare funds more efficient, the quality of services will also be improved (1) by establishing an efficient welfare network that facilitates access to information among interested ministries, (2) by preventing budgetary waste through continual assessment and evaluation of cost—benefit efficiency and the general quality of welfare operations, (3) by inducing the private sector to increase its participation in social welfare, and (4) by shifting more of the funding responsibility and more administrative operations to local governments.

2. Tax Justice Through Fair Taxation

2.1. Tax Justice is the Foundation of Productive Welfare

One of the core tenets of social welfare is to redistribute wealth to those who do not enjoy the benefits of a prosperous society. Providing the means to redistribute wealth is a primary function of taxation, and thus, tax justice lays the foundation for a productive welfare system and, ultimately, for social justice.

Article 38 of the Constitution states that "All citizens shall have the duty to pay taxes......." It is, thus, one of the four primary duties for Korean citizens. Anyone who holds Korean citizenship should pay taxes in accordance with his or her ability. If the Government wants citizens to voluntarily perform their duty to pay taxes, it should tax each citizen fairly, according to his or her financial position and should also allow the people who pay their taxes to enjoy the benefits of citizenship through the efficient use of tax collections.

Tax justice can be attained, not through the efforts of only one side, but by the exercise of reciprocal duties. One of the core concepts of productive welfare is that the Government must intervene in the market on behalf of the poor who have been excluded from the mainstream market process. In essence, government intervention is very similar to the redistribution of income through taxation. Intervention is, thus, the realization of tax justice that is implemented in the spirit of productive welfare.

2.2. Securing a Taxable Income Base

In the past, the Government used taxation as a means to fund economic growth without regard for the redistribution of income. In Korea, the tax-burden disparity between income-tax brackets has widened, causing conflict between upper- and lower-income people. Thus, there is little voluntary cooperation from the people to comply with tax laws.

Another problem is lax taxpayer bookkeeping. There is a propensity not to give or receive transaction receipts, which causes the tax base to be very weak because of low "reported" income. The tax compliance level is almost 95 percent for salaried wage earners, but for the self-employed, tax compliance can only be estimated at 30 to 50 percent, depending upon the type of business. In this way, those who do not honestly report their incomes transfer their tax burden to those in full compliance of the law.

The Government has begun to address the problem of tax collections. One step that the Government has taken to encourage the accurate reporting of income is to improve the transparency of transactions by encouraging consumers to use credit cards instead of cash. Another step taken by the

Government to improve transparency was taken in September 1999, when the Government allowed a new personal income tax deduction for the amount of total credit card purchases that exceeds 10 percent of a taxpayer's annual salary. The Government aims ultimately to make the tax base fair, rather than to merely relieve the tax burden of wage and salary earners. Introducing a lottery system, using credit card receipts, is another part of the plan. The Government hopes to accelerate the accurate reporting of self-employed income by encouraging consumers to favor the use of credit cards, rather than cash.

The current dual systems of simplified and special tax reporting components of the value-added tax (VAT) were introduced for small businesses having no bookkeeping capabilities. These small businesses constitute 60 percent of VAT taxpayers, but provide only 1.7 percent of all tax revenues. These tax provisions are often used by the high-income self-employed to avoid paying their fair share of taxes. To cope with this form of tax evasion, the Government will change "special" taxpayers to "simplified" taxpayers and change "simplified" status to "normal" status.

To minimize the effects of burdensome bookkeeping, the Government will prepare a stepwise taxpayer transition procedure to prevent the sudden increase of the tax burden on small businesses that will be caused by the change in VAT taxation categories. To accommodate the lowest income categories, businesses that earn less than 24 million won annually will continue to be exempt from paying taxes, so their tax burden will be unaffected by the tax reforms.

2.3. Increasing Tax Fairness Through Tax Reform

To reduce income inequality, the Government will raise the tax rate for high-income earners. Computerized techniques of tax auditing will be employed to improve the accuracy of tax audits. The scope of assessment will be extended to inheritance and gift taxes and will be modified to increase the tax burden of the rich. Unreported inheritances and gifts will be prevented by using new auditing techniques. To deal with those who have escaped paying the proper inheritance or gift tax because the statute of limitations (currently 15 years) has expired, the Government intends to duly revise the statute of limitations.

The Government will also extend the capital gains tax by assessing the capital gains acquired from the transfer of common stock at a progressive rate of 20 to 40 percent. The gift tax on the transfer of unrealized capital gains, usually share-price gains by formerly private companies that became publicly listed companies, is designed to thwart the illegal and irregular transfer of wealth through inheritance or gift giving. The Government also plans to adjust the special consumption tax base by excluding some popular and commonly used items.

To fully implement a fair tax system, a modern, computerized database, maintained by a consortium of national agencies and public organizations, will be coupled to the Tax Integration System (TIS) of the National Tax Administration, which will lay the foundation for the modernization of tax administration. The Government will also reintroduce the "global" income tax system t o clearly signal that the Government is determined to pursue equitable taxation.

Chapter 9

Forming a Community Based on Participation and Cooperation

To pursue both economic growth and social welfare, the welfare system must be overhauled to include democratic decision-making procedures, respect for the consumer's right to choose, and dissemination of shared policy objectives. Key to achieving these goals is the division of labor among the Government, local communities, businesses, and labor unions. The Government will be responsible for building public confidence through the implementation of democratic decision-making procedures and the local communities will be responsible for identifying and solving local problems. Businesses and labor unions will also share their responsibilities for establishing a well-developed welfare system. These and other non-government groups will be asked to participate in the Government's endeavor to develope welfare services in Korea.

1. Government: Encouraging Participation Through the Restoration of Public Confidence

Despite the high priority that has been placed on augmenting the welfare system, past administrations failed to achieve widespread public support nor positive results from their programs. This was primarily due to the lack of grass-roots involvement in defining policy objectives. Another prominent factor in previous disappointments in building a modern welfare system in Korea was that there did not exist an appropriate system to distribute services to the needy. To fashion an effective and efficient welfare system, trust between the Government and various constituencies in the private sector, for example private businesses, labor unions, local communities, civic groups, and individuals, must first be built. For successfully promoting quality welfare programs, the Government will attend to nurturing public confidence by building cooperative relationships between the public and private sectors.

1.1. Expansion of Private-Sector Participation in the Policymaking Process

In order to construct a welfare system based on participatory decision-making, the Government will involve all sectors of society at the policymaking level. In the past, local governments were bypassed in the determination of welfare -related policies, which limited the relevancy of some programs, ultimately resulting in the exclusion of some citizens from needed services or in the creation of duplicate services. To avoid such problems in the future, the Government plans to increase the participation of businesses and labor unions in the reforming and determination of the current welfare system for the purpose of better meeting the needs of welfare recipients.

1.2. Establishment of a Beneficiary-Oriented System

Meaningful results from these policies cannot be expected if there is no effective system to deliver welfare services. For instance, the proposed Minimum Living Standards Security Act, which intends to raise the standard of living for those at or below the poverty line, will be seriously hampered without a well-defined set of procedures to determine eligibility and to administer payments.

For building a welfare system that is responsive to the needs of the community, the Government will reform the currently "closed" system of administration to an "open" system of administration that encourages citizen participation. In opening the system, the central administrative organization will transfer a substantial set of organizational and budgetary authority to local governments for addressing problems locally. In order to escape from rigidity in budgetary and administrative structures, the autonomy of local authorities will be expanded and a comprehensive subsidy program that could include block grants will be aggressively pursued. The central government will install an information management system, establish standard evaluation procedures, and secure adequate funds for the equitable distribution of resources by geographic region.

Reform of the public welfare delivery system is crucial in securing the confidence of the private sector in the Government's ability to plan and implement productive policies. In line with this objective, the number of social workers and the quality of training will be greatly increased. Reform of the public welfare delivery system is aimed at providing user-friendly services and at eliminating duplicated services among various programs, such as unemployment, health, and social services that exist across ministerial and local agency jurisdictions.

1.3. Supporting Private-Sector Welfare Programs

Public-sector efforts cannot meet welfare needs alone. A complementary private-sector welfare system must also be developed to fully meet the welfare needs of the nation.

Support for existing groups, such as the Local Social Welfare Network, which includes regional private-sector groups, religious organizations, and citizen representatives, are deemed essential as an avenue for grass-roots participation.

Incentives to increase cooperation with the private sector in the implementation of welfare programs are another crucial pathway of involvement. Private-sector participation will be induced by endorsing the cooperation of for-profit and not-for-profit organizations as legitimate entities and by regularly supporting private-sector volunteer activities. The social "safety net" will be expanded through private- and public-sector participation, joint fundraising, and volunteer service activities. Current budgetary restrictions on procurements are expected to be alleviated by the establishment of the Self-help Assistance Fund.

2. Strengthening the Role of the Private Sector

Providing an adequate welfare program requires a basic change on the part of the private sector. The private sector, which was formerly regarded as a passive recipient of policy, must be allotted an active role as a partner in policymaking and implementation.

The main financial contributors to sound welfare, businesses and labor unions, must be encouraged to participate actively in determining key policies that would ensure efficient use of their welfare contributions. The diverse concerns of local communities, from social and civic groups to religious organizations, should be considered and addressed as policy issues. Partnership with the private sector should also complement public-sector efforts by providing voluntary involvement in the local community.

2.1. Labor Unions and Businesses: Private-Sector Partners of Productive Welfare

Cooperative bonds among the Government, labor, and business are the foundation for effective policymaking. Employers need to alleviate labor distrust by adopting transparent management procedures and by linking pay increases to the productivity of workers and the profitability of the firms. Labor, on the other hand, can undertake demo-cratic debate and equitable negotiations keeping in mind the development of both the business and the nation.

The Government must improve transparent reporting of social security contributions and tighten tax regulations to discourage the unreasonable amassing of wealth. These measures can contribute to the elimination of social discord resulting from the gap between the rich and poor. An added benefit of transparency and tighter tax regulations is the fostering of an environment of mutual trust between labor and management, which will alleviate discord between hourly workers and the self-employed.

Businesses and labor unions have already negotiated and implemented major policies in this direction during the process of overcoming the economic crisis. Their role in the future in promoting social objectives will be even more important. An effective welfare system is impossible without the active cooperation of both business and labor. Every business and every labor union must fulfill their respective social responsibilities to reduce unemployment and improve business productivity. Reemployment opportunities must also be expanded by increasing investments in job training and lifelong education, thus, assuring the development of human resources for the nation.

Business and labor will have to widen the scope of their activities from internal problem solving to policymaking. As members of their local communities, business and labor must share in the formation of policies that advance the development of their respective regional industrial economies.

To relieve the traditional antagonism between business and labor, there ought to be a mutual redirection of bipolar attitudes, a change in the "us and them" way of thinking. Within the framework of productive welfare, both entities will be partners in building a better society, the keyword being "we." Businesses and labor unions will both have to extend their responsibilities to help funding or to provide welfare and social services in their local communities as a way of returning the rewards of their work to society.

The Government must, thus, ensure the participation of both businesses and labor unions in the policy-drafting process and make possible their participation in a range of welfare related activities, including education.

2.2. Civic Groups

Civic groups increase the social awareness of problems associated with the alienated classes, which are easily missed or overlooked by Government or business. These civic groups are voluntary associations, which consist of ordinary citizens, that can wield much influence through their organized activities.

The activities of various civic groups differ by region in Korea and many of these groups are not yet sufficiently confident of their ability to implement programs. For civic groups to act as full partners in the welfare establishment, they need to improve their level of professionalism and organize into regional and national administrative units that democratically include all such organizations in the decision-making process.

The mobilization of local resources also needs to be initiated, for which the Government will build an infrastructure to support civic-group activities. Creativity in problem solving through grass-roots groups will be encouraged by the speedy passage of the proposed Non-Profit Private Sector Group Assistance Act. To further boost the vitality of socially responsible local civic groups, tax incentives will be granted to increase their contributions to effective welfare-related programs.

2.3. Local Communities and the Individual: Improving Quality of Life Through Joint Activities

The role of the Government is being redefined within the framework of productive welfare reform. The role of the individual citizen must also change. The time has come for citizens to take part as mature members of society by actively participating in volunteer activities and collectively solving problems in their local communities. The Government can help these local volunteer activities with funding, administrative guidance, access to information, and education of the public about welfare-related issues.

Enabling the widest possible range of participation by all members of society is necessary to affect meaningful, relevant welfare reform. Individuals, as well as organizations and the Government, must be active participants in welfare by volunteering their time and energy to solve their own local problems. As economic producers, labor and business must also help nurture relevant welfare programs with financial support and technical expertise. Civic groups can help by mobilizing their local communities to educate local residents and by administering local volunteer programs.

To fully exploit the energy and creativity of the people, the Government and the private-sector must agree on a common welfare vision and then work together to fulfil that vision. Only when they consistently work together, will that vision become a reality.